THE CRYING GAME

Neil Jordan is the author of *Night in Tunisia*, a collection of stories which won a Somerset Maugham Award, and two novels *The Past* and *The Dream of a Beast*. His films include *Angel*, which starred Stephen Rea, *Company of Wolves* which he wrote with Angela Carter and *Mona Lisa* which starred Bob Hoskins, Michael Caine and Cathy Tyson.

THE CRYING GAME

Neil Jordan

VINTAGE

First published 1993

3 5 7 9 10 8 6 4

© 1993 by Neil Jordan

Neil Jordan has asserted his
right under the Copyright, Designs and Patents Act, 1988
to be identified as the author of this work

First published in the United Kingdom in 1993 by Vintage
Random House, 20 Vauxhall Bridge Road, London SW1V 2SA

Random House Australia (Pty) Limited
20 Alfred Street, Milsons Point, Sydney,
New South Wales 2061, Australia

Random House New Zealand Limited
18 Poland Road, Glenfield
Auckland 10, New Zealand

Random House South Africa (Pty) Limited
PO Box 337, Bergvlei, South Africa

Random House UK Limited Reg. No. 954009

A CIP catalogue record for this book
is available from the British Library

ISBN 0 09 932711 2

Printed and bound in Great Britain by
Cox & Wyman Ltd, Reading, Berkshire

The Crying Game

an original screenplay

INTRODUCTION

I tend to write scripts as sparely as possible, for two reasons. Firstly, the barer the language is the easier it is to concentrate on the essentials when directing what you've written. And those essentials I would define as what is seen, what happens, and what is said. Secondly, because elaborate visual, psychological, or visceral description tends to confuse those you have to work with—designers, cinematographers, and, most importantly, actors. The kind of sentence that may be appropriate in a novel or a short story would be not only inappropriate, it would be misleading. To take an example from Kafka: 'As Gregor Samsa awoke one morning from uneasy dreams he found himself transformed in his bed into a gigantic insect.' One of the most beautiful and succinct sentences ever written, but one belonging to a world of realities that is most unhelpful to the filmmaker. The number of questions it raises are legion. It implies, for a start, a multitude of prior days on which Gregor Samsa woke up to find himself a human being. And assuming one could construct the insect that does justice to Kafka's imagination, how does one convey that this insect once was Gregor Samsa? How on earth does an insect wake up?

This is not to say that these problems are insurmountable, merely that the linguistic realities with which Kafka deals are light-years away from those the scriptwriter must handle. Which again, I would define as what is seen, what happens, and what is said. There are, however, linguistic pleasures to be gleaned from scriptwriting—apart from those one reads about in screenwriting manuals about dramatic structure, the 'arc' of the character (whatever that is), the first, second, and third act (why only three?), and so on. And those pleasures are to do with the application of language towards a quite specific purpose. When you strip it bare of all psychological implications and metaphoric weight, as you must, you are left with the heart of the matter: the accurate, succinct, and uncluttered description of what you wish to see on the screen. And for one who also writes prose, as I do, this can be as bracing as a cold shower on a December day.

Apart from language, of course, there is the story. And one could argue that the problems of narrative are the same for all fictions, written, spoken, or filmed. *The Crying Game* had a long gestation. I initially thought of the story after my first film, *Angel*, a story that arose out of the Northern Irish conflict, about a British soldier held hostage by an IRA activist. The situation had been dealt with twice before in Irish literature, by Frank O'Connor in a short story called 'Guest Of The Nation' and by Brendan Behan in a play called *The Hostage*. The attraction of such a theme for Irish writers, the friendship that develops between two protagonists in a conflict, that grows paradoxically deeper than any of their other allegiances, lies in the broader history of Anglo-Irish relationships: two cultures in need of each other, yet at war with each other. The fact that such a theme can be as relevant in the twenties, for O'Connor, and in the fifties, for Behan, as in the nineties, for me, says more than I want to ponder about the current state of things. O'Connor and Behan dealt with simple friendship between two men. Underlying this friendship lay an erotic possibility, a sense of mutual need and identification that could have provided salvation for their protagonists. That possibility remained subdued, and so both stories ended tragically. With *The Crying Game*, I brought the erotic thread to the surface. Instead of two, there were now three. A hostage, a captor, and an absent lover. The lover became the focus for the erotic subtext, loved by both men in a way they couldn't love each other. And the story ended with a kind of happiness. I say a kind of happiness, because it involved the separation of a prison cell and other more profound separations, of racial, national, and sexual identity. But for the lovers, it was the irony of what divided them that allowed them to smile. So perhaps there is hope for our divisions yet.

Neil Jordan

The
Crying
Game

CHARACTERS

(in order of appearance)

Jody	FOREST WHITAKER
Jude	MIRANDA RICHARDSON
Fergus	STEPHEN REA
Maguire	ADRIAN DUNBAR
Tinker	BREFFINI McKENNA
Eddie	JOE SAVINO
Tommy	BIRDIE SWEENEY
Dil	JAYE DAVIDSON
Jane	ANDREE BERNARD
Col	JIM BROADBENT
Dave	RALPH BROWN
Deveroux	TONY SLATTERY
Franknum	JACK CARR
Bar Performer 1	JOSEPHINE WHITE
Bar Performer 2	SHAR CAMPBELL
Judge	BRIAN COLEMAN
Security Man 1	RAY DE-HAAN
Security Man 2	DAVID CRIONELLY

EXTERIOR. CARNIVAL – DAY.

A loudspeaker playing Percy Sledge's 'When a Man Loves a Woman', as we see a carnival in the distance – with a Ferris Wheel turning round and round.

The song echoes round the carnival. Youths with cropped hair and tattoos shooting pellet guns. Kids whooping on a roller coaster.

A black man is by a stall, dressed in khaki. On his arm is an Irish girl with blond hair. The black man is drunk, and is tossing rings around a bowling pin.

JODY: And that's cricket, hon.

[*An attendant hands him the teddy bear. It looks ridiculous in his huge hands. He gives it to the girl.*]

JODY: You want it?

GIRL: Sure.

JODY: Doesn't matter if you don't.

[*He puts his arm around her and drags her on.*]

JODY: Jody won't be offended. What'd you say your name was?

GIRL: Jude.

JODY: Jude. Suits you, Jude.

JUDE: The teddy bear?

JODY: No, fuck the bear. The name. Jude. And it's June. Jude in June.

[*He comes to a small canvas tent with a sign on it – TOILET.*]

JODY: Gotta piss, Jude.

[*He holds her hand.*]

JODY: Don't run off, Jude.

JUDE: You don't know me, do you?

[JODY *walks inside the canvas flap and vanishes from sight. We can still see his hand, holding* JUDE's. *She leans against the canvas, looking bored.*]

JODY: [*inside*] What if I did?

3

JUDE: You'd know I wouldn't run off.

[*She stands there, listening to the sound of him urinate. Her eyes flick around the carnival. They settle on a tall dark-haired man in a dark jacket. He nods.*]

JODY: Never pissed holding a girl's hand, Jude.

JUDE: You didn't?

JODY: And you know what?

JUDE: Tell me, Jody.

[*He staggers out, buttoning up.*]

JODY: It's nice.

[*He goes to kiss her. She turns her head away.*]

JUDE: Not here.

JODY: Who gives a fuck.

JUDE: You never know.

[*She pulls him over toward the water.*]

JODY: I never know nothing.

JUDE: People. They could be looking.

[JODY *follows her, as she walks backward, drawing him on. He moves his hips to a song, as* JUDE *leads him over the beach, under a train trestle.*]

JUDE: Come and get me, soldier –

JODY: Whatever you say, Jude . . .

[*He sinks down on his knees toward her. She wraps her arms around his neck and kisses him.* JODY *writhes on top of her, fumbling with his belt.* JUDE *cocks one eye upward. A shadow falls across them.*]

[*Close on* JODY, *kissing her. A gun is put to his head. He turns around, drunkenly.*]

JODY: What the fuck –

[*The gun whacks him across the cheek and he falls sideways.*]

[JUDE *scrambles to her feet and darts like an animal through a field.*]

[JODY *feels his cheek. He can see her blond head vanishing among the fields. He looks up and sees a group of men around him. The tallest of them,* FERGUS, *cocks the gun.*]

INTERIOR. CAR – DAY.

A mini, driving down a country road. Two men *in the front, three in the back.*

On the floor of the car JODY *lies, with three pairs of feet on top of him, a black bag over his head and the barrel of a gun dangling close to his face.* FERGUS *holds the gun. He is smoking a cigarette. His movements are slow and somewhat innocent.*

FERGUS: So what's your name, soldier?

JODY: Fuck you.

FERGUS: Yeah.

EXTERIOR. SMALL FARMHOUSE – EVENING.

The car drives slowly up to a farmhouse. It has an incongruously large greenhouse attached to it. The car grinds to a halt and JODY *is dragged from it.*

INTERIOR. FARMHOUSE – NIGHT.

JODY *pulled through and tied to a chair.* MAGUIRE, *a small lean man, talks to him through the hood.*

MAGUIRE: The situation is simple. You're being held hostage by the Irish Republican Army. They've got one of our senior members under interrogation in Castleraigh. We've informed them if he's not released within three days, you'll be shot. You'll be treated as our guest until further developments. Have you anything to say?

[JODY *is motionless under the black hood.*]

FERGUS: Give him a cup of tea.

MAGUIRE: Do you want a cup of tea?

[*He still says nothing.*]

[*Dissolve.*]

[*All the men are drinking tea. The blond woman comes in with a plate and some food on it.*]

FERGUS: See does he want some.

JUDE: Do you want some food?

[JODY *sits as still as a grave, saying nothing.*]

[*Dissolve.*]

[*Late at night – it is dark. The men are sleeping.* FERGUS *is sitting by a chair, gun in his hand, watching the prisoner.* JUDE *comes in, with a flashlight.*]

FERGUS: Hey, Jude – what's he like?

JUDE: Horny bastard.

FERGUS: Did you give him it?

JUDE: There are certain things I wouldn't do for my country.

[*She points the flashlight at* JODY, *still motionless in the dark.*]

FERGUS: Have a look at him.

JUDE: Can't.

FERGUS: Poke him or something. See if he's still alive.

JUDE: He's all right.

FERGUS: Hasn't moved for twelve hours.

[*She flashes the light on him again.*]

FERGUS: Go on. Have a heart.

[*She moves over to him. She prods him in the legs with her foot. He doesn't move. Then she lifts the hood ever so slightly, to peer inside. Suddenly the man moves like lightning, jerking his head down so the hood comes off, throwing his body, tied to the chair, over* JUDE.]

JODY: You fucking bitch – you fucking whore –

[*He pins her to the ground, his body bent with the chair. He writhes on top of her in a grotesque parody of love. She is screaming and the room is alive, each man awake, grabbing guns, screaming. One of them switches the light on.*]

MAGUIRE: Turn the fucking thing off –

[*Close on* JODY's *face – looking at each one of them.*]

MAGUIRE: Turn it off – he's looking . . .

[*He shoots out the bare bulb and the room falls into darkness. Silence. Then we hear* JODY *laughing softly.*]

JODY: See, I never forget a face.

EXTERIOR. FARMHOUSE – NIGHT.

FERGUS *leads* JUDE *out a back door, holding her by the arm.*

FERGUS: You all right?

JUDE: Fucking animal.

[*She takes in huge gobs of air.*]

FERGUS: You don't know that.

JUDE: Fucking do. I had him all over me.

[*He touches her face.*]

FERGUS: Tough work, that.

JUDE: Someone's got to do it.

[*She rubs her hand on his chest.*]

JUDE: Nah, it was a breeze. Just thought of you.

[*She sidles closer, coming on to him.*]

JUDE: And you know the truth, Fergus? One of you made me want it . . .

[*She puts her lips to his neck.*]

FERGUS: Which one?

[*She doesn't answer. They embrace.*]

EXTERIOR. FARMHOUSE – MORNING.

A hot summer's day. There are tall hedges all around the house. FERGUS *leads* JODY, *still bound and hooded, over toward a greenhouse.*

INTERIOR. GREENHOUSE – DAY.

Dusty tomato plants and vines everywhere. Broken glass. The sun pouring through. FERGUS *leads* JODY *over to a wrought iron chair and sits him in it. He sits opposite, gun on his lap.* FERGUS *takes some sandwiches out of a brown paper bag. He holds one out toward him.*

FERGUS: Eat something, would you?

JODY: Can't.

FERGUS: What do you mean you can't?

JODY: Can't eat through a canvas bag.

[FERGUS *walks over to him, lifts the hood up so his mouth is revealed, and pushes the sandwich toward his lips.* JODY *eats, slowly.*]

JODY: This is a farce, man.

FERGUS: How is it a farce?

JODY: I seen your fucking face.

FERGUS: So, what do I look like?

7

JODY: You're the one about five ten with the killer smile and the baby face.

FERGUS: Am I?

JODY: Yeah. And the brown eyes.

[FERGUS *pushes the last crumbs of the sandwich toward* JODY's *mouth*.]

JODY: You're the handsome one.

[JODY *eats the last bits*.]

JODY: Thank you, handsome.

FERGUS: My pleasure.

EXTERIOR. FARMHOUSE – DAY.

JUDE *makes her way from the door toward the greenhouse. She is carrying a pot of tea and two cups.*

INTERIOR. GREENHOUSE – DAY.

It is sweltering now in the greenhouse. Close on JODY's *cowled head. The hood is drenched with sweat.*

JODY: I can't fucking breathe, man. Be a Christian, will you?

[JUDE *comes into view*.]

JODY: Tell him to take the hood off, honey . . .

[JUDE *says nothing. Lays the tea on the ground*.]

FERGUS: How did you know it was her?

JODY: I can smell her perfume.

[JUDE *pours out the tea*.]

JUDE: See, if we took the hood off, we'd have to shoot you. As it is, you've got a fifty-fifty chance.

JODY: Thought you liked me, bitch.

JUDE: It was fun while it lasted.

JODY: Nice lady.

[*His breathing becomes laboured*.]

JODY: Please, man, I'm suffocating in here.

FERGUS: Can't we take it off?

JUDE: Have to check with himself.

[FERGUS *gives her the gun*.]

FERGUS: You look after him.

[JODY's *head follows* FERGUS *while he leaves.*]
JODY: Don't leave me with her, man. She's dangerous . . .
    [JUDE *smiles, holding the gun on her lap.*]

INTERIOR. FARMHOUSE – DAY.

FERGUS *enters.* MAGUIRE *and the others.* MAGUIRE *has a newspaper, which has a headline regarding the kidnapping.*
MAGUIRE: Made the front page. They'll move now, the fuckers.
FERGUS: Request permission to take the hood off, Tommy.
MAGUIRE: Why would you do that?
FERGUS: The poor whore's suffocating in the heat.
MAGUIRE: So?
FERGUS: And anyway, he's seen our faces.
MAGUIRE: You sure?
FERGUS: He described me down to a T. Knows what Jude looks like.
    [MAGUIRE *reads the paper.*]
FERGUS: Tommy –
MAGUIRE: You're his keeper. If you don't mind him seeing you, I don't mind. But you're the only one he looks at.
FERGUS: Thanks.
MAGUIRE: It's your decision.

INTERIOR. GREENHOUSE – DAY.

JUDE, *drinking tea, looking at* JODY *sweating.* FERGUS *enters. He puts his arm casually around her.*
FERGUS: Leave us, Jude.
JUDE: My pleasure.
    [*She goes.* FERGUS *walks to* JODY *and slowly takes the hood off.* JODY *looks up at him, his face bathed in sweat. He breathes in mighty gulps of air. He smiles.*]
JODY: Thank you, soldier.
    [FERGUS *smiles.*]
JODY: Never thought fresh air would taste this good.
    [FERGUS *pours out a cup of tea and brings it to his lips.*]
JODY: Now, if you took the ropes off, I'd be able to feed myself.

9

FERGUS: No fucking way.

JODY: Only joking.

[FERGUS *drinks*.]

JODY: You know, I was wrong about one thing.

FERGUS: What's that?

JODY: Five ten. Brown eyes. But you're no pinup.

FERGUS: No?

JODY: Nope. Not handsome at all.

FERGUS: You trying to hurt my feelings?

JODY: No. It's the truth.

FERGUS: Well, I could say the same about you.

JODY: Could you?

FERGUS: But I won't. We're more polite around these parts.

JODY: So I've noticed.

[FERGUS *looks at him.* JODY *isn't smiling anymore.* FERGUS *goes back to his seat and drinks his tea. He fingers the gun on his lap.*]

JODY: Hey –

FERGUS: What is it now?

JODY: You're going to have to do it, aren't you?

FERGUS: Do what?

JODY: Kill me.

FERGUS: What makes you think that?

JODY: They're going to let that guy die. And you're going to kill me.

FERGUS: They won't let him die.

JODY: You want to bet?

FERGUS: I'm not a gambling man.

JODY: And even if he doesn't die – you can't just let me loose.

FERGUS: Why can't we?

JODY: Not in your nature.

FERGUS: What do you know about my nature?

JODY: I'm talking about your people, not you.

FERGUS: What the fuck do you know about my people?

JODY: Only that you're all tough undeluded motherfuckers. And that it's not in your nature to let me go.

FERGUS: Shut the fuck up, would you?

JODY: And you know the funny thing?

10

FERGUS: No, what's the funny thing?

JODY: I didn't even fancy her.

FERGUS: Didn't look like that to me . . .

JODY: She's not my type.

[*He looks at* FERGUS.]

JODY: C'mere.

FERGUS: No.

JODY: Ah, c'mere. I want to show you something.

FERGUS: What?

JODY: My inside pocket.

[FERGUS *holds the gun to his face. He fishes inside Jody's inside pocket.*]

JODY: Take out the wallet.

[FERGUS's *hand emerges with a wallet.*]

JODY: Open it.

[*Close on the wallet. Credit cards, army identification photograph.*]

JODY: Inside. There's a picture.

[FERGUS *takes out a picture. It is of* JODY, *in cricket whites, smiling, holding a bat.* FERGUS *smiles.*]

JODY: No, not that one. There's another.

[FERGUS *takes out another picture of Jody and of a beautiful black woman, smiling.*]

JODY: Now *she's* my type.

FERGUS: She'd be anyone's type.

JODY: Don't you think of it, fucker.

FERGUS: Why not?

JODY: She's mine. Anyway, she wouldn't suit you.

FERGUS: No?

JODY: Absolutely not.

FERGUS: She your wife?

JODY: Suppose you could say that.

[JODY *chuckles.*]

FERGUS: You make a nice couple.

JODY: Don't I know it.

FERGUS: So what were you fucking around for, then?

JODY: You fuckers set me up. That bitch –

FERGUS: She's a friend of mine –

11

JODY: Okay. That nice lady. Meets me in a bar. I'm saying what the fuck am I doing here anyway. She buys me a drink. She holds my hand. I'm looking at her saying I don't like you, bitch. But what the fuck. Maybe I'll get to understand.

FERGUS: What?

JODY: What the fuck I am doing here.

FERGUS: What the fuck were you doing here?

JODY: I got sent.

FERGUS: You could have said no.

JODY: Can't. Once I signed up.

FERGUS: Why did you sign up?

JODY: It was a job. So I get sent to the only place in the world they call you nigger to your face.

FERGUS: Shouldn't take it personally.

JODY: [*He imitates a Belfast accent*] 'Go back to your banana tree, nigger.' No use telling them I came from Tottenham.

FERGUS: And you play cricket?

JODY: Best game in the world.

FERGUS: Ever see hurling?

JODY: That game where a bunch of paddies whack sticks at each other?

FERGUS: Best game in the world.

JODY: Never.

FERGUS: The fastest.

JODY: Well, in Antigua cricket's the black man's game. The kids play it from the age of two. My daddy had me throwing googlies when I was five. Then we moved to Tottenham and it was something different.

FERGUS: How different?

JODY: Toffs' game there. But not at home.

[FERGUS *looks at him.*]

JODY: So when you come to shoot me, Paddy, just remember you're getting rid of a shit-hot bowler.

FERGUS: I'll keep that in mind.

[*He keeps looking at him.*]

FERGUS: And by the way, it's not Paddy. It's Fergus.

[JODY *smiles.*]

JODY: Nice to meet you, Fergus.

FERGUS: My pleasure, Jody.

EXTERIOR. GREENHOUSE – NIGHT.

FERGUS *runs* JODY *outside, holding the gun to his head.*

FERGUS: Take it easy, now. Just go slow. Down by that tree.

JODY: Tree.

JODY: Loosen my hands.

FERGUS: Can't.

JODY: Well then, you're going to have to take my dick out, aren't you?

[FERGUS, *in the dark, stands motionless, looking at him.*]

JODY: Come on, man, I'm going to wet my pants!

[FERGUS *turns him around and unzips his fly.*]

JODY: Take the fucker out, man, I'm dying –

[FERGUS *takes* JODY'*s penis out.*]

[JODY *takes two steps toward the wall.*]

JODY: I gotta lean forward or I'll dribble all over me – hold my hands –

[FERGUS *holds his hands from behind, so* JODY *can lean forward.* JODY *now pisses with immense relief.*]

JODY: Now, that was worth waiting for.

FERGUS: Hurry up, would you?

JODY: These things take time, Fergus.

[*He shakes his body.*]

JODY: It's amazing how these small details take on so much importance . . .

[*He steps back.*]

JODY: Now put it back in.

FERGUS: Give us a break.

JODY: It's only a piece of meat, for fuck's sake!

[FERGUS *puts* JODY'*s penis back in his pants.*]

JODY: No major diseases.

[FERGUS *zips him up.*]

JODY: Case of the clap two years ago. Crabs in Ulster. But all in all it's served me well.

FERGUS: Shut up, would you?

JODY: I'm sorry. Didn't mean to offend you, Fergus.

13

[FERGUS *leads him back toward the greenhouse.*]

INTERIOR. GREENHOUSE – NIGHT.

FERGUS *leads* JODY *back to his chair.*
JODY: Fergus?
FERGUS: Yeah?
JODY: Thanks. I know that wasn't easy for you.
  [*He begins to laugh.*]
FERGUS: The pleasure was all mine.
  [FERGUS *begins to laugh, without knowing why.*]

EXTERIOR. FARMHOUSE – NIGHT.

MAGUIRE, *walking out of the house, woken by the sound of laughter.*

INTERIOR. GREENHOUSE – NIGHT.

JODY, *still laughing. Suddenly the hood is slammed back over his head.*
  [MAGUIRE, *standing there in the dark, looking at* FERGUS.]
MAGUIRE: What the fuck is this?
JODY: Nothing, man. He just had to help me pee –
MAGUIRE: What the fuck is this?
FERGUS: It's nothing. He's just got a sense of humour, that's all.
MAGUIRE: You're on duty. Keep your fucking mouth shut.
FERGUS: Yes, sir.
MAGUIRE: Go in and get some sleep.
  [FERGUS *gets up slowly, walks toward the door.*]
JODY: Yeah. Get some sleep.

EXTERIOR. FARMHOUSE – NIGHT.

FERGUS, *walking toward the house. He looks back and sees the figures of* MAGUIRE *and* JODY, *in the dark, in absolute silence.*

INTERIOR. FARMHOUSE – NIGHT.

FERGUS *sleeping*.

INTERIOR. GREENHOUSE – NIGHT.

JODY *sleeping*. MAGUIRE *sitting with an Armalite in his hands, watching him*.

EXTERIOR. FARMHOUSE AND FIELDS – DAY.

The sun coming up over the low hills around the farmhouse.

INTERIOR. GREENHOUSE – DAY.

FERGUS *enters, with a tray and some breakfast*. MAGUIRE *is sitting where he sat before, stock-still*.

FERGUS: Did he talk?

[MAGUIRE *shakes his head*.]

FERGUS: Didn't make you laugh?

[MAGUIRE *shakes his head*.]

FERGUS: Here. Have some breakfast.

[*He hands* MAGUIRE *a plate*. JODY *stirs*.]

JODY: Good morning, Fergus?

[MAGUIRE *looks hard at him*.]

MAGUIRE: So he knows your name?

FERGUS: I told him.

MAGUIRE: Are you all there?

[*He rises, and drags* FERGUS *out the door*.]

MAGUIRE: You'll have minimal contact with the prisoner, do you hear me?

FERGUS: Yes.

MAGUIRE: And do you know why?

FERGUS: Why?

MAGUIRE: Because tomorrow we might have to shoot him, that's why.

[MAGUIRE *goes back to the house*.]

INTERIOR. GREENHOUSE – DAY.

JODY *sitting with the hood on again.* FERGUS *enters.*

JODY: They giving you trouble, Fergus?

[FERGUS *says nothing. He takes a plate and brings it toward* JODY.]

JODY: It happens. Y'see, there's two kinds of people. Those who give and those who take.

[FERGUS *lifts up Jody's hood to expose his mouth and begins to feed him.*]

JODY: Ah, take the thing off, man.

[FERGUS *says nothing and keeps feeding him.*]

JODY: It's okay. I understand. Don't mind if I prattle on, do you?

[FERGUS *shakes his head and says nothing.*]

JODY: I will take it by your silence that you don't.

[*He eats.* FERGUS *feeds himself, then feeds more to* JODY.]

JODY: Two types, Fergus. The scorpion and the frog. Ever heard of them?

[FERGUS *says nothing.*]

JODY: Scorpion wants to cross a river, but he can't swim. Goes to the frog, who can, and asks for a ride. Frog says, 'If I give you a ride on my back, you'll go and sting me.' Scorpion replies, 'It would not be in my interest to sting you since as I'll be on your back we both would drown.' Frog thinks about this logic for a while and accepts the deal. Takes the scorpion on his back. Braves the waters. Halfway over feels a burning spear in his side and realizes the scorpion has stung him after all. And as they both sink beneath the waves the frog cries out, 'Why did you sting me, Mr Scorpion, for now we both will drown?' Scorpion replies, 'I can't help it, it's in my nature.'

[JODY *chuckles under his hood.*]

FERGUS: So what's that supposed to mean?

JODY: Means what it says. The scorpion does what is in his nature. Take off the hood, man.

FERGUS: Why?

JODY: 'Cause you're kind. It's in your nature.

[FERGUS *walks toward him and pulls off the hood.* JODY *smiles up at him.*]

JODY: See? I was right about you.
FERGUS: Don't be so sure.
JODY: Jody's always right.

INTERIOR. GREENHOUSE – LATE AFTERNOON.

Both men dozing in the heat.
JODY: Where would you most like to be now, man?
FERGUS: Doesn't matter where.
JODY: Come on, man. If this shit was all over.
FERGUS: Having a pint in the Rock.
JODY: You lack imagination, Fergus. Think of something more
    alluring.
FERGUS: Like what?
JODY: Like having a pint in the Metro –
    [FERGUS *laughs*.]
FERGUS: Having two pints in the Rock.
JODY: Having a pint in the Metro, and Dil's having a margarita.
FERGUS: Who's Dil?
JODY: My special friend.
FERGUS: Oh, yeah.
JODY: We got simple tastes, you and me.
FERGUS: The best.
JODY: But you fellas never get a break, do you?
FERGUS: Do you?
JODY: Oh, yes. We do a tour of duty and we're finished. But you
    guys are never finished, are you?
FERGUS: We don't look on it like that.
JODY: I've often wondered how you do it.
FERGUS: Depends on what you believe in.
JODY: What do you believe in?
FERGUS: That you guys shouldn't be here.
JODY: It's as simple as that?
FERGUS: Yes.
    [JUDE *enters*.]
JUDE: Put that thing back on him, Fergus.
FERGUS: He's hot.
JUDE: Doesn't matter if he's hot. Just cover the fucker up.
JODY: Have you no feelings, woman?

17

JUDE: You shut your face –
  [*She pulls the hood down over him.*]
JUDE: You're heading for trouble, Fergus –
JODY: He's a good soldier, Jude.
  [*She whacks him with a pistol.*]
JUDE: I said shut the fuck up –
JODY: He believes in the future –

INTERIOR. GREENHOUSE – NIGHT.

JODY, *sitting in the hood.* FERGUS *lifts it a bit;* JODY's *mouth, with blood now in his lips.*
FERGUS: Is it bad?
JODY: No. Not bad. Women are trouble, you know that, Fergus?
FERGUS: I didn't.
JODY: Some kinds of women . . .
FERGUS: She can't help it.
JODY: Dil wasn't trouble. No trouble at all.
FERGUS: You liked her?
JODY: Present tense, please. Love her. Whatever she is. I'm
  thinking of her now, Fergus. Will you think of her too?
FERGUS: Don't know her.
JODY: Want you to do something, Fergus.
FERGUS: What?
JODY: If they kill me –
FERGUS: Don't think that way.
JODY: But they will. As sure as night follows day. They have to. I
  want you to find her out. Tell her I was thinking of her.
  [FERGUS *is moved. He can't reply.*]
JODY: See if she's all right.
FERGUS: I don't know her.
JODY: Take her picture. C'mere.
  [FERGUS *walks toward him.*]
JODY: Take it. In the inside pocket.
  [*Their faces, close to each other as* FERGUS *searches out her
  picture.*]
JODY: Take the whole lot. I won't need it.
FERGUS: I told you not to say that –

JODY: Go to Millie's Hair Salon in Spitalfields. Take her to the Metro for a margarita. Don't have to tell her who you are. Just tell her Jody was thinking –

FERGUS: Stop it –

[*The door opens.* MAGUIRE *is there, with another.*]

MAGUIRE: Volunteer?

[FERGUS *turns toward him.*]

MAGUIRE: We need you inside.

[FERGUS *walks toward* MAGUIRE *and the other* MAN *walks forward, takes his seat.* FERGUS, *unseen by* MAGUIRE, *puts the wallet in his pocket.*]

INTERIOR. FARMHOUSE – NIGHT.

MAGUIRE, JUDE, FERGUS, *and the* OTHERS.

MAGUIRE: We've had word. They've used every trick in the book on him. He's starting to talk. You're going to have to do it in the morning.

[FERGUS *looks at him and nods.*]

MAGUIRE: Are you all right about this?

FERGUS: I volunteered, didn't I?

MAGUIRE: Good. I've been worried about you for the last few days.

JUDE: Not the only one –

MAGUIRE: Shut up, Jude. You best get some sleep tonight, Fergus.

[FERGUS *says nothing, just stands there.*]

MAGUIRE: Fergus. Go to sleep.

FERGUS: Peter.

MAGUIRE: What?

FERGUS: Request permission to guard the prisoner tonight –

JUDE: Are you fucking crazy? Don't let him, Peter.

MAGUIRE: I said shut up, Jude!!!

[*He puts his arm on* FERGUS's *shoulder.*]

MAGUIRE: Why do you want to do that?

FERGUS: Would make me feel better about it.

MAGUIRE: You're sure you want to do that?

FERGUS: I'm sure.

MAGUIRE: Okay. You're a good man, Fergus.

[FERGUS *leaves.*]

INTERIOR. GREENHOUSE – NIGHT.

FERGUS *takes his place in the chair beside* JODY.

[JODY *begins to laugh under the hood. It turns into the sound of crying.*]

FERGUS: Don't.

JODY: I'm sorry.

[*The crying stops.*]

JODY: Help me.

FERGUS: How can I?

JODY: I don't know. Just help me. Give me a cigarette.

[FERGUS *takes out a cigarette, lights it, and lifts up Jody's hood so he can smoke.*]

JODY: Don't even smoke, you know that? It just seemed the right thing to do.

[FERGUS *watches him puff the cigarette, the hood just above his lips.* JODY *coughs, but keeps the cigarette in his lips.* FERGUS *gently takes the cigarette from his mouth.*]

FERGUS: Go to sleep now.

JODY: I don't want to sleep. Tell me something.

FERGUS: What?

JODY: A story.

FERGUS: Like the one about the frog?

JODY: And the scorpion. No. Tell me anything.

FERGUS: When I was a child . . .

JODY: Yeah?

FERGUS: I thought as a child. But when I became a man I put away childish things . . .

JODY: What does that mean?

FERGUS: Nothing.

JODY: Tell me something, anything.

FERGUS: When I was a kid my uncle had a carnival in Monaghan. I used to get free rides on the swings.

JODY: And?

FERGUS: Only when the day was finished and the place near empty. So I'd swing as the sun went down.

JODY: And?
FERGUS: Nothing. That's it. That was my little bit of bliss.
JODY: And that's the story?
FERGUS: Yes.
   [FERGUS *is silent; his eyes wet.*]
JODY: Not a lot of use, are you, Fergus?
FERGUS: Me? No, I'm not good for much . . .

EXTERIOR. FIELDS – MORNING.

The farmhouse covered in mist. The sun coming through it.

EXTERIOR. GREENHOUSE – MORNING.

MAGUIRE *opens the door to the greenhouse and clicks the chamber of his gun.* FERGUS *has a gun in his hand. He checks the chamber.*

   [FERGUS *takes* JODY, *whose hands are still tied behind his back, by the elbow.*]
FERGUS: Stand up, now –
   [JODY *rises.* FERGUS *leads him through the door, past* MAGUIRE.]
MAGUIRE: I wish to say on behalf of the Irish Republican Army –
   [FERGUS *turns with sudden fierceness.*]
FERGUS: Leave him be –
   [*He pulls* JODY *through the fields.*]

EXTERIOR. TREES – MORNING.

FERGUS *pushing* JODY *through a copse of trees, the gun at his back.*
JODY: Take the hood off, Fergus –
FERGUS: No.
JODY: I want to see a bit. Please, please. Don't make me die like an animal.
   [FERGUS *pulls the hood off.* JODY *looks around him. He has a cut lip where* JUDE *struck him.*]
   [FERGUS *prods him on with the gun.* JODY *stumbles forward.* FERGUS *is all cold and businesslike.*]

JODY: I'm glad you're doing it, do you know that, Fergus?

FERGUS: Why?

JODY: 'Cause you're my friend. And I want you to go to the Metro —

FERGUS: Stop that talk now —

JODY: Hurling's a fast game, isn't it, Fergus?

FERGUS: The fastest.

JODY: Faster than cricket?

FERGUS: Cricket's in the halfpenny place.

JODY: So if I ran now, there's no way I'd beat you, is there?

FERGUS: You won't run.

JODY: But if I did . . . you wouldn't shoot a brother in the back —

[JODY *suddenly springs, and, despite the fact that his arms are tied behind him, he is off like a hare.* FERGUS *screams in fury after him.*]

FERGUS: Jody!!!

[FERGUS *aims, then changes his mind and runs.*]

FERGUS: You stupid bastard —

JODY: What you say, faster?

FERGUS: I said you bastard — stop —

JODY: Got to catch me first —

[FERGUS *gains on him — stretches his arm out — but* JODY *sprints ahead again — as if he has been playing with him. He laughs in exhilaration.* FERGUS *pants behind him, wheezing, almost laughing.*]

JODY: Used to run the mile, you know — four times round the cricket pitch — what was that game called?

FERGUS: Hurling —

JODY: What?

FERGUS: Hurling —

[JODY *runs, whipping through the trees — always ahead of him.*]

JODY: Come on, Fergie — you can do it — a bit more wind —

[FERGUS *grabs his shoulder and* JODY *shrugs it off, gaining on him again.*]

JODY: Bit of fun, Fergus, eh?

[*And suddenly the trees give way,* JODY *turns, laughing, to* FERGUS.]

JODY: Told you I was fast —

[FERGUS *is panting, pointing the gun at* JODY.]
JODY: Don't do it.
    [*And suddenly a Saracen tank whips around the corner, hits* JODY *with the full of its fender. His body flies in the air and bounces forward as another tank tries to grind to a halt and the huge wheels grind over him.*]
    [FERGUS, *hidden by the trees, screaming, 'No – !' He almost moves forward, then sees soldiers spilling from the tank around the body.* FERGUS *turns and runs.*]

EXTERIOR. TREES – DAY.

FERGUS *whipping through the trees, his body crouched low as he runs.*

INTERIOR. GREENHOUSE – DAY.

TINKER *sitting in the greenhouse. A helicopter screams into view through the panes and automatic fire comes from it, shattering every pane in seconds and tearing* TINKER *to bits.*

INTERIOR. FARMHOUSE – DAY.

Bullets whipping through every window, taking chunks from the masonry, tearing the walls apart. MAGUIRE, JUDE, *and the* OTHERS *on the floor, scrambling for weapons.*

EXTERIOR. TREES – DAY.

FERGUS *runs, hearing the gunfire. He veers left down to a small stream and splashes down it, through overhanging branches till eventually he is hidden from sight.*

EXTERIOR. CARNIVAL ON THE MONAGHAN BORDER – DAWN.

A row of swing boats over nondescript fields. One of them is swinging gently.

[*An* OLD MAN *comes from a caravan carrying a water pail. He walks between the swingboats. A hand comes from one of them and stops him.* FERGUS *gets out of the swingboat. The* OLD MAN *embraces him.*]

TOMMY: Fergus!

FERGUS: You're back in the pink, Tommy? How're you keeping?

INTERIOR. CARAVAN – DAY.

The OLD MAN *pouring whiskey into a teacup.*

TOMMY: You'll notice I've asked you nothing.

FERGUS: That's wise, Tommy.

TOMMY: All right, then. I like to be wise.

[*He pours* FERGUS *more whiskey.*]

TOMMY: So what do you need, Fergus?

FERGUS: Need to go across the water.

TOMMY: Do you now.

FERGUS: Need to lose myself awhile.

TOMMY: Aha.

[*He puffs.*]

[*He looks at* FERGUS *and lights a cigarette.*]

EXTERIOR. DUBLIN BAY – EVENING.

The ferry, churning into the sunset.
Fade to black.

INTERIOR. BUILDING SITE – DAY.

Fade up into an elegant, empty Georgian room, covered in clouds of dust. A figure among the clouds of dust, hacking at a wall with a sledgehammer. It is Fergus, dressed in labourer's overalls, covered in dust. He is knocking the bricks from an outer wall. He works furiously and relentlessly, like a machine.

We see the wall, with the hammer striking it. One brick falls away, then another. Daylight pours through the clouds of dust and the growing hole.

FERGUS's *face, as he works.*

24

The hole. More bricks falling away. Through the clouds of dust and the streams of daylight we now see a patch of green.

FERGUS's *face, working. His rhythm slows.*

The hole. More bricks fall away. Then the hammer stops. The dust begins to clear.

His face.

The jagged hole. The dust drifts across it, revealing a cricket pitch, with tiny sticklike figures running on the green.

Through the haze of dust we see a bowler, in slow motion, rubbing the ball on his crotch, then running to bowl, dreamlike, in slow motion.

FERGUS, *staring.*

EXTERIOR. HOUSE – DAY.

We see the house from the cricket pitch, a Georgian mansion covered in scaffolding with workmen crawling all over it.

INTERIOR SITE – DAY.

FERGUS, *by the hole in the wall. He has the soldier's wallet in his hand, open to reveal the picture of the woman.*

INTERIOR. HOSTEL – DAY.

FERGUS *dressing. He puts on a cheap suit, like any country boy in a big city. He takes Jody's wallet from the trousers of his overalls. He flips it open, sees the picture of the soldier, and of* DIL. *He puts it in the pocket of his suit.*

EXTERIOR. STREET – DAY.

FERGUS *walking down a street looking for an address. Some distance down the street is a sign – Millie's Unisex Hair Salon.*

EXTERIOR. STREET – DAY.

FERGUS, *standing as the crowds go by him, looking in the window.*

25

He has the picture in his hand. We see DIL *from his point of view, then* FERGUS *walks inside.*

INTERIOR. HAIR SALON – DAY.

FERGUS *enters. The door gives a loud ping.*

A GIRL: We're closing.

    [*She leaves the salon.*]

DIL: You want something in particular?

FERGUS: Just a bit of a trim . . .

    [DIL *checks her watch and stubs out a cigarette*]

DIL: Come on . . .

    [*She gestures toward a chair.* FERGUS *sits down. She comes toward him and fiddles with his hair.*]

    [*She pushes his head back into a basin behind him. She begins to knead his hair in hot water and shampoo.*]

DIL: Someone recommend you?

FERGUS: In a way.

DIL: Who?

FERGUS: Guy I work with.

DIL: What's his name?

    [FERGUS *can't think of an answer. The hands with the purple nails run over his scalp.*]

FERGUS: Doesn't the water get to your nails?

DIL: What's it to you?

FERGUS: Nothing.

    [*She begins to cut.*]

DIL: You American?

FERGUS: No.

DIL: Not English.

FERGUS: No.

DIL: Scottish?

FERGUS: How'd you guess?

DIL: The accent, I suppose.

FERGUS: And what's it like?

DIL: Like treacle.

    [*She imitates his accent saying it.* FERGUS *laughs.*]

DIL: Nice laugh.

[*A mirror, with a clock on it, reading half-past six.* DIL *raises* FERGUS's *head up, with his new-cut hair and holds a mirror up behind his head so he can see the back. He looks like a young London stockbroker. The hair salon around them is empty.*]

DIL: That should make her happy.

FERGUS: Who's she?

DIL: Don't know. Who is she?

EXTERIOR. HAIR SALON – EVENING.

FERGUS *emerges from the shop. He takes one last look through the window where* DIL *is taking off her smock, touching up her hair, etc. It is as if she has forgotten all about him. He walks off through the crowds and then ducks into a doorway.*

The doorway of the shop. DIL *comes out, dressed in a pair of high heels, a very short skirt, different, more raunchy clothes on her than we saw inside. She locks the glass door and walks down the street, across the road, and into a pub called the Metro.* FERGUS *follows.*

INTERIOR. METRO – EVENING.

Half full, with an after-work crowd. DIL *makes her way through it.*

BARMAN: Hi, Dil.

DIL: Hiya, hon.

[*She sits down at the bar.* FERGUS *comes toward the bar and takes a seat.*]

BARMAN: What'll it be?

FERGUS: A bottle of Guinness.

[DIL, *looking at* FERGUS.]

DIL: See that, Col?

COL: See what, Dil?

DIL: He gave me a look.

COL: Did he?

[FERGUS *blushes. He buries himself in his drink.*]

DIL: Just cut his hair, you know.

COL: Yeah?

DIL: What you think?

COL: Nice.

[FERGUS *throws his eyes toward her again. She has her face turned away, but sees him in the mirror.*]

DIL: There, he did it again.

COL: Saw that one.

DIL: What would you call it?

COL: Now, that *was* a look.

[*She eyes* FERGUS *in the mirror.*]

DIL: Ask him to ask me what I'm drinking.

[*The* BARMAN, *with infinite weariness, approaches* FERGUS.]

COL: She wants to know do you want to know what she's drinking.

[FERGUS *is about to talk when she pipes up.*]

DIL: A margarita.

[*The* BARMAN *mixes it. She stares at the mirror, staring at* FERGUS, *who is trying to avoid her eyes. The* BARMAN *hands her the drink.*]

DIL: Now he can look.

[*The* BARMAN *hands* FERGUS *a chit. He pays it, still trying to avoid her eyes.*]

DIL: Ask him does he like his hair, Col.

COL: She wants to know, sir, do you like your hair.

FERGUS: Tell her I'm very happy with it.

DIL: He's Scottish, Col.

COL: Scottish?

FERGUS: Yeah.

DIL: What'd he say, Col?

COL: He agreed that he was.

DIL: What do you think his name is?

COL: I've no thoughts on the matter.

FERGUS: Jimmy.

DIL: Jimmy?

COL: That's what he said. Jimmy.

DIL: Hi, Jimmy.

FERGUS: Hiya, Dil.

[*A burly man sits down beside her. He puts his hand on her knee.*

MAN: Sing the song, Dil –
  [*She slaps the hand away.*]
DIL: Fuck off, Dave.
DAVE: C'mon, babe! You know what I like . . . Easy!
  [*She turns back to* FERGUS *and finds his seat empty.*]

EXTERIOR. METRO – NIGHT.

FERGUS, *standing across the road from the pub. He is sweating.*
DIL *comes out of the pub. She looks this way and that, as if
searching for* FERGUS. FERGUS *stands back into a shadow.* DAVE,
*the burly man, comes out. He grabs her by the elbow. She shrugs
him off. She walks off.* DAVE *follows, grabs her by the elbow
again. The sense of an old argument.* DAVE *suddenly strikes her
across the face with his open palm. She leans her head against a
wall.* DAVE *then puts his arms around her, consoles her.*

EXTERIOR. STREET – NIGHT.

DAVE *walking, holding* DIL *by the arm. The street is dilapidated,
full of squats. They stop outside a door.* DIL *opens the door with a
key from her purse and they both walk inside.*
  FERGUS *stands there, observing.*
  A light comes on in an upstairs room. DIL *enters; we see her
shadow in silhouette behind the curtain and the shadow of* DAVE
*coming in behind her. He begins to remove her blouse. She stands
absolutely still as he does so.*
  FERGUS *backs away, then walks off.*

EXTERIOR. CRICKET PITCH – NIGHT.

JODY *as a bowler, running in slow motion, toward the camera. He
releases the ball; we see* FERGUS *in bed, breathing heavily.*

INTERIOR. SITE – NEXT DAY.

FERGUS, FERGUS *takes a break and watches the batsman hit a ball.
He imitates the batsman's motion with his sledgehammer. Then a
voice interrupts him.*

DEVEROUX: So Pat's a cricket fan, eh?

[FERGUS *turns. We see* TRISTRAM DEVEROUX, *a young Sloane type in a three-piece suit, whose house it is. Beside him is* FRANKNUM, *the cockney foreman.*]

FERGUS: It's not Pat. It's Jim.

DEVEROUX: Jim, Pat, Mick, what the fuck. Long as you remember you're not at Lords.

FERGUS *resumes work.*

INTERIOR. METRO – NIGHT

It is now crowded with people, black, white, punky and street-chic, a lot of leather. All the women are heavily made-up. Someone is singing from the tiny stage and rows of cheap coloured bulbs are flashing around it.

From the way FERGUS *walks through, it is obvious he has never been here at night. He seems most out of place in his cheap suit, making his way through the crowd to the bar.*

AT THE BAR.

FERGUS *looks through the odd crowd, but can't find* DIL. COL, *the* BARMAN, *sees him and smiles.*

COL: So can we consider you a regular, sir?

FERGUS: Is that good or bad?

COL: Well, you get to say, *The usual, Col.* Things like that.

[COL *pushes a coloured cocktail with one of those Japanese umbrellas toward him.*]

COL: So let's call this the usual.

FERGUS: Thanks.

[FERGUS *reaches for his wallet to pay, but Col interrupts.*]

COL: No, no. It's on me.

[FERGUS *tries to pretend he's familiar with the drink, and by implication, whatever are the norms of the place. He lifts the glass to his mouth, but the umbrella keeps getting in the way.*]

COL: Take it out, if you want.

[FERGUS *takes out the umbrella. He holds it in one hand and drinks with the other.*]

COL: You came to see her, didn't you?
   [FERGUS *shrugs. He takes out a cigarettte. A guy in leather to his left smiles at him.*]
COL: Something I should tell you. She's –
FERGUS: She's what?
   [*The* BARMAN *looks up toward the stage.*]
COL: She's on.

THE JUKEBOX

A hand presses a button. The needle selects a disc. A song by Dave Berry, 'The Crying Game'.

AT THE BAR.

FERGUS *looks up. We see* DIL, *standing by the jukebox, swaying slightly. She seems a little drunk. She mimes to the song. She mouths the words so perfectly and the voice on the song is so feminine that there is no way of knowing who is doing the singing. She does all sorts of strange movements, as if she is drawing moonbeams with her hands.*

   The crowd seems to know this act. They cheer, whether out of approval or derision we can't be sure.

   FERGUS *watching.*

   DIL *singing, noticing him. She comes to the end of the song. The crowd cheers.*

   FERGUS, *watching her make her way through the crowded bar, toward him.*
DIL: He's still looking, Col.
COL: Persistent.
DIL: Good thing in a man.
COL: An excellent quality.
DIL: Maybe he wants something.
COL: I would expect he does.
DIL: Ask him.
COL: Ask him yourself.
   [*She looks at* FERGUS *directly, sits down next to him.*]
DIL: So tell me.

31

[FERGUS *says nothing. He shrugs.*]

DIL: Everybody wants something.

FERGUS: Not me.

DIL: Not you. How quaint. How old-fashioned and quaint. Isn't it, Col?

[COL *shrugs.*]

DIL: You old-fashioned?

FERGUS: Must be.

[*The burly* MAN *comes up to her.*]

MAN: Got the money, Dil.

DIL: Fuck off, Dave.

DAVE: You fucking promised.

DIL: Did I?

DAVE: You fucking did.

[*He suddenly jerks her roughly off the stool, spilling her drink.*

DAVE: Didn't you? Well, come on!

[*He drags her through the crowd. In the mirror,* FERGUS *watches them go. The* BARMAN *eyes him.*]

COL: It takes all types.

FERGUS: So who's he?

COL: He's what she should run a mile from.

FERGUS: Then why doesn't she?

COL: Who knows the secrets of the human heart.

[FERGUS *suddenly stands and makes his way to the door.*]

EXTERIOR. PUB – NIGHT.

FERGUS *comes out. The black bouncer is there, but there is no sign of* DIL. *He walks a few yards and hears voices down an alley. He looks up it.*

POV – ALLEY.

We see DIL *pushing* DAVE *away. He grabs her, turns her roughly.*

DAVE: Don't be like that –

DIL: You heard me –

[*She beats his arms away. Money falls on the ground. She*

staggers away from him. He picks up the money, then runs after her.]

DAVE: Got very fucking grand, haven't we –
[*He tries to pull her back.*]

DAVE: Talk to me, you bitch –
[*They both bump into* FERGUS, *who just stands there and doesn't move an inch. She smiles.*]

DIL: Hi.

FERGUS: Hi. You forgot your bag.
[*He holds it up to show her.*]

DAVE: Who the fuck is he?

DIL: Jimmy.

DAVE: It's him, isn't it?

DIL: Maybe.
[DAVE *eyes* FERGUS. FERGUS *grabs his wrists and upends him on the ground.*]

DIL: See, they get the wrong idea.

DAVE: [*From the ground*] Cunt.
[FERGUS *puts his foot on his neck.*]

FERGUS: What was that?

DIL: They all get the wrong idea.

DAVE: Cunt. Scrag-eyed dyke cunt.

DIL: Charming.
[DAVE *grabs for her ankle. She kicks his hand away.* FERGUS *press down his foot. He looks to* DIL.]

FERGUS: What'll I do?

DIL: Break his neck.
[FERGUS *presses his foot.*]

DIL: No, don't.
[*She bends low to* DAVE.]

DIL: He's going to take his foot off slowly, David. Then you're to go home, like a good boy. You hear me?

DAVE: Cunt.
[*But his voice is softer.* FERGUS *removes his foot.* DIL *grabs his arm.*]

DIL: Come on, honey.
[*She draws him away.*]

EXTERIOR. METRO – NIGHT.

[*They walk out of the alley.*]
FERGUS: You all right?
DIL: Yes, thank you.
FERGUS: So what was that all about?
DIL: He wants me to perform for him.
FERGUS: Perform?
DIL: You know.
  [FERGUS *walks in silence for a while.*]
FERGUS: You on the game?
DIL: God no. I'm a hairdresser.
  [FERGUS *looks back.* DAVE *is rising.*]
FERGUS: He's getting up.
DIL: You can't leave me then, can you?

EXTERIOR. STAIRCASE OUTSIDE DIL'S FLAT.

FERGUS *and* DIL *climb slowly upstairs.*
DIL: You want me to ask you in, right?
FERGUS: No, I didn't –
DIL: But I'm not cheap, you know that? Loud, but never cheap.
  [*There is a movement lower down the staircase. We see* DAVE, *holding his neck.*]
DAVE: Fucking dumb dyke carrot cunt.
  [DIL *leans close to* FERGUS.]
DIL: If you kissed me, it would really get his goat.
  [*She tilts up her face.* FERGUS *kisses her, tenderly.*]
DIL: Now, if you asked me to meet you tomorrow, it would really drive him insane.
FERGUS: Where?
DIL: Half-five. At Millie's.
  [*She goes in and closes the door.* FERGUS *stands and looks down at* DAVE, *who turns to leave.*]

EXTERIOR. HAIR SALON – DAY.

[DIL *walks out of the salon, smiling, and walks toward* FERGUS.]
DIL: Give me that look again.

34

FERGUS: Which look?

DIL: The one you gave me in the Metro.

[FERGUS *takes a bunch of flowers from behind his back. She holds them, with theatrical feeling.*]

DIL: Darling, you shouldn't have.

[*She laughs and leans toward him and kisses him, bending one foot to reach him, in a classically old-fashioned way. The girls inside the salon pull back a curtain, and they all clap.*]

FERGUS: What's that about?

DIL: They're jealous.

FERGUS: Why?

DIL: I wonder.

[*She takes his arm and walks off with him.*]

INTERIOR. INDIAN RESTAURANT – NIGHT.

FERGUS *and* DIL *looking at their menus. A waiter places drinks on their table, then leaves.*

DIL: Now's the time you're meant to do something, isn't it?

FERGUS: Like what?

DIL: Make a pass or something. Isn't that the way it goes?

FERGUS: Must be.

EXTERIOR. STREET – NIGHT.

They are walking in an alleyway toward her house.

DIL: You got a special friend, Jimmy?

FERGUS: How special?

DIL: You want one?

[*And suddenly a car drives very fast toward them, headlights on.* FERGUS *pulls her into a doorway to avoid it.*]

FERGUS: Jesus Christ!

DIL: Jesus.

[*The car continues down the road, stops, and then screeches off, and just sits there, headlights toward them.*]

FERGUS: That Dave?

DIL: The things a girl has to put up with.

[*She looks down toward where the car has pulled away.*]

DIL: I'm frightened, Jimmy. That's not like him.

EXTERIOR. DIL'S FLAT.

A car pulls up behind DIL *and* FERGUS.

DIL: Piss off, Dave!

FERGUS: Tough guy, huh? Are you going to be all right on your own?

DIL: I'm not on my own, am I?

[*She touches his cheek.*]

DIL: Come on up, would you?

INTERIOR. DIL'S FLAT – NIGHT.

DIL *comes in in the darkness.* FERGUS *stands like a shadow in the doorway. The light comes on; she takes off her raincoat.*

DIL: Won't hurt you to come in.

[FERGUS *enters slowly. He looks around the room; there is an exaggerated femininity about everything in it.*]

DIL: Would you like a drink?

FERGUS: Yes, please.

DIL: What'll it be?

FERGUS: Whiskey.

[*She goes into a small kitchen.* FERGUS *looks at the mantlepiece and sees a picture of* JODY. *The camera tracks into the* SOLDIER'*s smiling face. Then into* FERGUS'*s face. His reverie is broken by the sound of a voice outside –* DAVE'*s.*]

[*She comes through with two drinks.*]

FERGUS: Someone out there.

DIL: Jesus fucking Christ.

[*She opens the window door, and we see* DAVE *on the street, in a neck brace.*]

DIL: Hey, Stirling fucking Moss –

DAVE: It's Dave.

[*She goes back into the room and begins taking things up.*]

DAVE: Talk to me, Dil –

DIL: Sure, Dave –

DAVE: Please, Dil –

[*She flings things down: men's clothes, leather trousers, a suitcase, a teddy bear.*]

DIL: Take your clothes.

DAVE: Don't throw my clothes out the window!

DIL: Fuck off back to Essex!

DAVE: Fucking mad!

[FERGUS *looks to the man down in the street, a parody of rejection with his things in his arms.*]

DIL: Take your fucking goldfish, too!

[DIL *grabs a large goldfish bowl and flings it down. The bowl breaks to bits on the pavement. Goldfish thrash around in the street.*]

DAVE: You fucking bitch!

[*He tries to pick up the flapping fish in his hands.*]

DAVE: Murderer!

[*Upstairs,* DIL *closes the window shut.*]

DIL: Sorry.

[*She hands* FERGUS *a glass.*]

DIL: How'd he drive with his neck in a brace?

FERGUS: Must be in love to manage that.

DIL: Doesn't know what the word means.

[FERGUS *stands with his drink and walks slowly round the room. There is a curtained closet with clothes inside it. He looks through the curtain and can see a pair of cricket whites inside.*]

FERGUS: He lived here with you?

DIL: Tried to. Sit down, will you?

[FERGUS *walks past the photograph and sits down. He looks from her to the picture.*]

FERGUS: What about him?

[*He nods toward the picture. She looks down into her drink.*]

DIL: He was different.

FERGUS: How different?

DIL: As different as it's possible to be.

FERGUS: Tell me about him.

DIL: No.

[*She leans forward.*]

FERGUS: Shouldn't I go?

DIL: Yes.

[*And they fall into one another's arms. She stretches up with her whole body over him. They grow suddenly and violently passionate.*]

[*They fall into the cushions of the couch onto the floor. The photograph above them seems to smile. He draws up her dress with his hands. She suddenly pulls away.*]

DIL: No –

FERGUS: Did you do that to him?

[*She comes up toward him once more. She puts her mouth close to his ear.*]

DIL: You want to know how I kissed him?

FERGUS: Yes . . .

DIL: Are you jealous of him?

FERGUS: Maybe.

DIL: That's good . . .

[*She opens the buttons on his shirt and her mouth travels down his chest.* FERGUS *tries to draw her up toward him, but her hand reaches up to his mouth and presses his head back while her other hand undoes his pants.*]

EXTERIOR. NIGHT.

JODY *as bowler, in white cricketer's uniform.*

INTERIOR. DIL'S FLAT.

Picture of DIL *and* JODY, *smiling.*

[FERGUS *has his head back. There are tears in his eyes.*]

FERGUS: What would he think?

DIL: Can't think. He's dead. In Ireland. He was a soldier. Went there like a fool.

FERGUS: Do you miss him?

DIL: What do you think?

FERGUS: I think you do.

DIL: [*Dreamily*] You say that like a gentleman.

FERGUS: Do I?

DIL: Like you're concerned.

DIL: But you can't stay, you know that?

FERGUS: Didn't think I could.

DIL: A real gentleman . . .

[*She embraces him.*]

FERGUS: Shouldn't you be in mourning?

DIL: I am.

[*She sits down in front of the mirror.* FERGUS *leaves. She reapplies her lipstick.*]

INTERIOR. METRO – NIGHT.

SINGER *in a blue dress.* DIL *and* FERGUS *by the bar. Both drinking drinks with umbrellas.* DAVE *comes up behind them with his neck brace.*

DAVE: Look, I'm sorry.

DIL: Fuck off, Dave.

DAVE: No, I won't fucking fuck off. Said I'm sorry, didn't I?

DIL: Yeah. I heard. You hear, Jimmy?

[FERGUS *nods. He stands.* DAVE *steps two feet back.*]

FERGUS: I was only going to ask her for a dance.

[FERGUS *takes* DIL's *arm.*]

FERGUS: Shall we?

[*The slim black woman is singing.*]

[*As they circle, people begin to look at them admiringly.* DIL *holds her cheek close to his.*]

FERGUS: Did he come here too?

DIL: Is this an obsession of yours?

FERGUS: Maybe.

DIL: He did sometimes.

FERGUS: Did he dance with you?

[DIL *doesn't answer. Looks at him out of the corner of her eye.*]

DIL: So what do you want with me, Jimmy?

FERGUS: Want to look after you.

DIL: What does that mean?

FERGUS: Something I heard someone say once.

[*She draws back and looks at him.*]

DIL: You mean that?

FERGUS: Yeah.

[*She dances closer.*]

DIL: Why?

FERGUS: If I told you, you wouldn't believe me.

[*In the bar, people singing along with the music.* COL *sings.* DAVE *sitting at the bar, sulking.*]

DIL: You're not having me on, are you? 'Cause Dil can't stand that.

FERGUS: No.

[*She puts her cheek against his.* DAVE *at the bar, slams his drink down.*]

DIL: And she does get very upset . . .

[*On the stage the act finishes.* DIL *draws him back to the bar.*]

AT THE BAR.

COL, *the barman, pours her drink.*

DIL: One for him, too.

[COL *pours and smiles.*]

DIL: Drink.

FERGUS: What is this?

DIL: I'm superstitious. Drink.

[*He drinks. He grimaces. She throws it back in one.*]

DIL: Can't leave me now.

FERGUS: Aha.

DIL: The thing is, can you go the distance?

FERGUS: Depends what it is.

DIL: No, depends on nothing.

[*She takes the bottle herself and fills their glasses. She slams it back. He sips.*]

DIL: In one.

[*She tilts his glass back. He swallows it in one.*]

INTERIOR. HER FLAT – NIGHT.

She enters; FERGUS *walks in slowly. He looks from the cricket whites to the photographs.*

DIL: What you thinking of, hon?

FERGUS: I'm thinking of your man.

DIL: Why?

FERGUS: I'm wondering why you keep his things.

DIL: Told you, I'm superstitious.

[*She turns toward him and undoes her hair. It falls around her shoulders.*]

FERGUS: Did he ever tell you you were beautiful?

DIL: All the time.

[FERGUS *runs his hand down her throat.*]

DIL: Even now.

FERGUS: No . . .

DIL: He looks after me. He's a gentleman too.

[*She draws him behind a curtain toward the bed, pulls him down. They kiss passionately.*]

DIL: Give me one minute.

[*She walks into the bathroom.* FERGUS *lies there, looking at the picture, listening to the sound of running water. She comes out then, dressed in a silk kimono. She looks extraordinarily beautiful. He reaches out his hand and grasps hers. He draws her toward him. He begins to kiss her face and neck.*]

FERGUS: Would he have minded?

[*She murmurs no. His hands slip the wrap down from her shoulders.*]

[*Close on his hands, travelling down her neck, in the darkness. Then the hands stop. The kimono falls to the floor gently, with a whisper. The camera travels with it, and we see, in a close-up, that she is a man.*]

[FERGUS *sits there, frozen, staring at her.*]

DIL: You did know, didn't you?

[FERGUS *says nothing.*]

DIL: Oh my God.

[*She gives a strange little laugh, then reaches out to touch him.* FERGUS *smacks the hand away.*]

FERGUS: Jesus. I feel sick —

[*He gets up and runs to the bathroom. She grabs his feet.*]

DIL: Don't go, Jimmy —

[*He kicks her away. He runs into the bathroom and vomits into the tub.*]

[*She crouches on the floor.*]

DIL: I'm sorry. I thought you knew.

41

[*He retches again.*]

DIL: What were you doing in the bar if you didn't know?

DIL: I'm bleeding . . .

[*She lights a cigarette.*]

[FERGUS *runs the taps. He washes his face, rinses his mouth.*]

DIL: It's all right, Jimmy. I can take it. Just not on the face.

[FERGUS *slams the door shut. She is sitting on the couch, the kimono round her once more, looking very much like a woman. A trace of blood on her mouth.*]

DIL: Y'see, I'm not a young thing any longer.

DIL: Funny the way things go. Don't you find that, Jimmy? Never the way you expected.

[FERGUS *comes out of the bathroom.*]

FERGUS: I'm sorry.

[*She looks up. Some hope in her face.*]

DIL: You mean that?

[*And he makes to go. She grabs him to stop him.*]

DIL: Don't go like that. Say something . . .

[*He pulls away from her. She falls to the floor.*]

DIL: Jesus.

[*He drags himself away and runs down the stairs.*]

INTERIOR. FERGUS' FLAT.

FERGUS *in bed. Flash to shot of blackness,* JODY *in cricket whites, throwing the ball up & down in his hand.*

INTERIOR. METRO – NIGHT.

The place is hopping. FERGUS *enters. He now sees it as he should have seen it the first night – as a transvestite bar. He makes his way through the crowds. All the women too-heavily made-up. Some beautifully sleek young things he looks at he realizes are young men. He makes his way to the bar where* DIL *is sitting, nursing a drink with an umbrella in it. Her face is bruised. She is wearing dark glasses.*

As he walks toward her she sees him in the mirror. She talks to COL, *the barman.*

DIL: He's back, Col.

COL: Hi.

DIL: Don't want any of those looks, Col. They don't mean much.

COL: Stop it, Dil –

DIL: No. Tell him to go fuck himself.

[FERGUS *sits.* COL *turns to him.*]

COL: She wants me to tell you go fuck yourself.

FERGUS: I'm sorry.

[*There is a tear running down her cheek, under the dark glasses.*]

DIL: Tell him to stop messing Dil around –

FERGUS: Dil –

DIL: Tell him it hurt –

FERGUS: I have to talk to her, Col –

COL: Says he's got to talk to you –

[FERGUS *touches her arm.*]

FERGUS: Come on, Dil –

DIL: Where?

[*She whips her arm away.*]

DIL: Tell him again, Col. Go fuck himself –

[*She walks into the crowd, toward the door.*]

[FERGUS *leaves.*]

EXTERIOR. STREET – NIGHT.

FERGUS, *walking outside Dil's place. The blinds in her room are down and the light is on inside. We see her outline, pacing up and down behind the blinds, smoking a cigarette. The song 'The Crying Game'.*

FERGUS *stands beneath her doorway, scribbles a note, and sticks it in the letter box.*

EXTERIOR. CRICKET PITCH – DAY.

A MAN *removes a large six from a huge scoreboard with a pole and replaces it with a number nine.*

Below the scoreboard we can see DIL *walking across a lawn toward the building, where* FERGUS *is working.*

INTERIOR. SITE – DAY.

FERGUS, *fitting a new window into the finished wall. On the pitch we see the cricketers, distorted through the moving glass of the window. Across the pitch* DIL *walks, with a lunch basket in her hand, dressed in a very short skirt with high heels. As she approaches the site a chorus of whistles breaks out.*

FERGUS, *hearing the whistling, stares out. He sees* DIL *moving toward the site. He drops the window and the glass shatters. As the whistles continue, we see* DIL *in the site's lift, which rises up. We see* DEVEROUX *and* FRANKNUM *climbing up a ladder toward* FERGUS.

DEVEROUX: How much did that frame cost, Mr Franknum?

FRANKNUM: Two hundred quid, Mr Deveroux.

DEVEROUX: Your Pat just cost me two hundred quid.

FERGUS: Sorry.

DEVEROUX: Sorry won't bring the bloody thing back, will it, Mr Franknum?

FRANKNUM: Not in my experience.

DEVEROUX: Off his wages.

FERGUS: Do you mean that?

DEVEROUX: He wants to know do I mean that.

FRANKNUM: I'm sure you do, Mr Deveroux.

DEVEROUX: Bloody right I do . . .

[*Through this conversation* FERGUS *can hear the chorus of wolf whistles increasing. He looks out the gap where the window should be and sees* DIL *in the lift. The labourers whistle at her, looking up her skirt, etc.*]

[*She passes by a gap in the wall and blows a kiss at him.*]

DEVEROUX: Is that his tart? Does Pat have a tart?

FERGUS: She's not a tart.

DEVEROUX: No, of course not, she's a lady.

FERGUS: She's not that either.

[FERGUS *walks out of the room.*]

[FERGUS *walks round the scaffolding.* DIL *sees him and waves, sits on some bricks and opens the hamper.*]

DIL: Darling –

[*She is acting bright and businesslike, like any wife. She is wearing dark glasses to cover the bruise on her face. She pecks him on the cheek.*]

DIL: Never let the sun go down on an argument, Jody used to say.

FERGUS: What you doing here?

DIL: Got your note. So let's kiss and make up, hon.

FERGUS: Don't call me that.

DIL: Sorry, darling.

FERGUS: Give it over, Dil –

DIL: Apologies, my sweet.

[FERGUS *smiles in spite of himself.*]

DIL: That's more like it, dear. Have a cuppa.

[*She takes out a thermos and pours him some tea.*]

FERGUS: You're something else, Dil, you know that?

DIL: Never said a truer word.

[*She hands him a neatly cut sandwich.*]

DIL: See, I was always best looking after someone. Must be something in the genes.

FERGUS: Must be.

DIL: And the fact that you didn't know is basically the fault of yours truly. And even when you were throwing up, I could tell you cared.

FERGUS: You could?

DIL: Do you care, Jimmy?

FERGUS: Sure I do.

DIL: You mean that?

FERGUS: Yeah. I care, Dil.

[*She lowers her head.*]

FERGUS: You crying, Dil?

[*He removes her glasses and looks at her moist eyes.*]

DIL: I'm tired and emotional.

FERGUS: You're never going to let up, are you?

DIL: No.

[*She says this softly, as if she really means it.* FERGUS *hears a wolf whistle. He looks over her shoulder and sees all the workers staring at him. He looks from them to* DIL, *her face tilted upward toward him, as if waiting to be kissed.*]

DIL: Ignore them, hon. Think of them as dross.

FERGUS: Told you not to call me that.

[*She smiles. He smiles.*]

[*Then he hears a voice behind him.*]

DEVEROUX: Do it on your own time, Paddy.

FERGUS: What?

DEVEROUX: Whatever it is she does for you.

[FERGUS *looks from* DIL *to* DEVEROUX.]

FERGUS: If I was her I'd consider that an insult.

DEVEROUX: Consider it how you want. Just get that bloody tart out of here.

[FERGUS *stands up suddenly. He speaks quietly.*]

FERGUS: Did you ever pick your teeth up with broken fingers?

[DEVEROUX *stares, suddenly chilled.*]

DEVEROUX: What's that supposed to mean?

FERGUS: It's a simple question.

[DEVEROUX *says nothing.* FERGUS *looks down to* DIL.]

FERGUS: Come on, dear.

[*He holds out his arm.* DIL *gathers up her things and takes it. Her face is wreathed in a smile.*]

DIL: He didn't answer, honey —

[FERGUS *walks her down the scaffolding ramp. As they pass the workers, she whispers:*]

DIL: My, oh my, Jimmy, how gallant.

FERGUS: Shut up.

DIL: Made me feel all funny inside.

FERGUS: I said stop it.

EXTERIOR. SITE.

FERGUS *and* DIL *descend from the site on the lift.*

DIL: Ask me to meet you again, Jimmy.

FERGUS: You think that's wise?

DIL: Nothing's wise.

[*The lift stops with a thud.*]

FERGUS: I didn't mean to hit you.

DIL: I know that.

FERGUS: Kind of liked you as a girl.

DIL: That's a start.

FERGUS: So I'm sorry.

DIL: Make it up to me, then.
FERGUS: How?
DIL: Ask to meet me again.
FERGUS: Will you meet me again?
DIL: When?
FERGUS: Whenever. Tonight.

[*She leans forwards and kisses him.* FERGUS *hears a wail of catcalls behind him. He watches* DIL *go as the lift takes him back up to the site.*]

EXTERIOR. HAIR SALON – EVENING.

FERGUS, *outside the hair salon.* DIL, *inside, is throwing off her smock and walking toward him. All the* GIRLS *are smiling.* FERGUS *looks from* DIL *to the* GIRLS *as they approach.*]
FERGUS: Do they know?
DIL: Know what, honey?
FERGUS: Know what I didn't know. And don't call me that.
DIL: Can't help it, Jimmy. A girl has her feelings.
FERGUS: Thing is, Dil, you're not a girl.
DIL: Details, baby, details.
FERGUS: So they do know.
DIL: All right, they do.

[*She takes his arm as they walk off.*]
FERGUS: Don't.
DIL: Sorry.
FERGUS: I should have known, shouldn't I?
DIL: Probably.
FERGUS: Kind of wish I didn't.
DIL: You can always pretend.
FERGUS: That's true.
FERGUS: Your soldier knew, didn't he?
DIL: Absolutely.
FERGUS: Won't be quite the same though, will it?
DIL: Are you pretending yet?
FERGUS: I'm working on it.
DIL: That's a start.

[FERGUS *hears a car following them, and turns around to look.*]

47

FERGUS: There's Dave. He knew too.

DIL: Stop it, Jimmy.

FERGUS: Am I becoming repetitious?

DIL: A little.

FERGUS: Sorry.

[*They reach her door. The car stops.*]

FERGUS: Don't ask me in.

DIL: Please, Jimmy.

FERGUS: No. Can't pretend that much.

DIL: I miss you, Jimmy.

FERGUS: Should have stayed a girl.

DIL: Don't be cruel.

FERGUS: Okay. Be a good girl and go inside.

DIL: Only if you kiss me.

[FERGUS *kisses her. He looks at her open lips as if in disbelief at himself.*]

FERGUS: Happy now?

DIL: Delirious.

INTERIOR. HOSTEL – NIGHT.

FERGUS *walks into the room and turns on a small desk-light. Then he hears a voice.*

JUDE: Hello, stranger.

[*He sees* JUDE *sitting in the corner. Her hair is now dark brown.*]

JUDE: You vanished.

[*He stares at her, says nothing.*]

JUDE: What was it, Fergus? Did you blow the gaff on us or did you just fuck up?

FERGUS: Leave me alone, Jude.

JUDE: No. That's the last thing I'll do. You never asked what happened.

FERGUS: I heard.

JUDE: Eddie and Tinker died.

FERGUS: I know.

JUDE: Maguire and me got out by the skin of our teeth. No thanks to you.

JUDE: What you think of the hair?

FERGUS: Suits you.

[*She walks round the room.*]

JUDE: Aye, I was sick of being blond. Needed a tougher look, if you know what I mean.

[*She lies down on the bed beside him and puts her hand on his crotch.*]

JUDE: Fuck me, Fergus.

[*He takes her hand away.*]

JUDE: Am I to take it that's a no?

[*She runs her finger up and down his face.*]

JUDE: We had a court-martial in your absence. They wanted to put a bullet in your head. I pleaded for clemency. Said we should find out what happened first. So what did happen?

FERGUS: He ran. I couldn't shoot him in the back. I tried to catch him. He made it to the road and got hit by a Saracen.

JUDE: So you did fuck up.

FERGUS: Yes.

JUDE: But you know what the thing is, Fergus?

FERGUS: What is the thing?

JUDE: You vanished quite effectively. Became Mister Nobody. And you've no idea how useful that could be.

FERGUS: What do you mean?

JUDE: We've got some plans here. And we'll need a Mister Nobody to execute them.

FERGUS: No way, Jude. I'm out.

JUDE: You're never out, Fergus.

[*She looks at him hard. He looks away.*]

JUDE: Maybe you don't care whether you die or not. But consider the girl, Fergus. The wee black chick.

[*He leaps up from the bed.*]

FERGUS: Leave her out of this.

JUDE: Jesus, Fergus, you're a walking cliché. You know we won't leave her out of this. But I'm glad to see you care.

[*She brings her lips close to his so they touch.*]

JUDE: And I must admit I'm curious.

[*He grabs her hair and pulls her head back.*]

FERGUS: What the fuck do you know, Jude?

[*She pulls a gun and sticks it between his teeth.*]

JUDE: You fucking tell me, boy —

[FERGUS *stares at her. Then says quietly:*]

FERGUS: She's nobody. She likes me.

JUDE: So I suppose a fuck is out of the question. Keep your head down, Fergus. No sudden moves. And not a whisper to her. You'll be hearing from us.

[*She kisses him briefly, with the sun at his temple.*]

JUDE: Keep the faith.

[*She goes.* FERGUS *stands in the darkness.*]

EXTERIOR. HAIR SALON — EVENING.

FERGUS, *walking toward the hair salon, flowers in his hand.*

He stands outside watching, the flowers behind his back. Then the chair turns and we see it is Jude.

FERGUS *freezes. He sees* JUDE *looking at him, smiling brightly, then talking back to* DIL.

INTERIOR. HAIR SALON — EVENING.

JUDE: He your boyfriend?

[JUDE, *turning in the chair.*]

JUDE: Lucky you.

INTERIOR. INDIAN RESTAURANT — NIGHT.

DIL: Carnations.

FERGUS: What?

DIL: He'd bring me carnations.

FERGUS: So I got it wrong, then.

DIL: Not at all, honey.

FERGUS: Don't.

DIL: Okay.

[*She smiles brightly at something behind* FERGUS. *He turns and sees* JUDE *is there.* FERGUS *stands, suddenly.*]

[*He throws some money on the table, grabs her arm, and frog-marches her out.*]

FERGUS: Come on.

DIL: Why, honey –
DIL: You gonna tell me why?
FERGUS: No.
  [*As they pass* JUDE, *she smiles.*]

EXTERIOR. INDIAN RESTAURANT – NIGHT.

Outside the restaurant. FERGUS *marches* DIL *away.*
DIL: What's wrong, Jimmy? Tell me what's wrong –
FERGUS: Not here.
  [*They pass out of shot. In the background we see* JUDE *rising.*]

INTERIOR. METRO – NIGHT.

DIL *and* FERGUS *making their way to their seats at the bar.*
DIL: You gonna tell me what it is?
  [*A figure sitting down at the bar. It is* JUDE.]
JUDE: What was it?
DIL: You know her, Jimmy?
JUDE: Jimmy, is it? Do you know me, Jimmy?
FERGUS: Dil, this is Jude.
DIL: You following me?
JUDE: Yeah. Just checking. He being nice to you, Dil?
DIL: Ever so nice. Aren't you, Jimmy?
JUDE: That's good. I'm glad. Young love, as they say.
DIL: Absolutely. The younger the better. Doesn't come your way
  much, I suppose.
JUDE: Don't go looking for it, Dil.
DIL: Well, maybe you'll get lucky. Someday.
JUDE: A bit heavy on the powder, isn't she, Jimmy?
DIL: A girl has to have a bit of glamour.
JUDE: Absolutely. Long as she can keep it. Isn't that right,
  James . . .
  [*She leaves.* DIL *watches her go.*]
DIL: It's her, isn't it?
FERGUS: What's her?
DIL: She's the thing you had to tell me.
FERGUS: Kind of.

DIL: I'm sorry, you know that? I'm really sorry.
  [*She looks at* COL.]
DIL: You see that, Col?
COL: Saw it, Dil.
DIL: Fuck it, is what I say.
COL: Yeah. Fuck it, Dil.
DIL: Fucking men, Col.
COL: Fuck 'em.
  [*There are tears in her eyes. She stands.*]
DIL: And fuck you, Jimmy —
  [*She staggers out of the pub.* FERGUS *sits there. There is an expression in* COL's *eyes that makes him feel very, very small.*]
COL: You could always make it up to her.
FERGUS: How?
COL: When a girl runs out like that, she generally wants to be followed.
FERGUS: She's not a girl, Col.
COL: Whatever you say.
  [*But* FERGUS *rises and walks out.*]

EXTERIOR. METRO – NIGHT.

A figure standing down the alleyway, smoking. FERGUS *looks toward it, but* JUDE *is standing there, waiting.*
JUDE: She went that way —
  [JUDE *grabs his arm.*]
JUDE: But you come with me.
  [*She draws him down an alley where the same car is waiting. They get inside.*]

ANOTHER CAR – BY THE PUB.

DIL, *standing in the shadows of a taxi watching* FERGUS *and* JUDE *getting in the car.*

INTERIOR. CAR – NIGHT.

In the moving car. JUDE *is driving,* MAGUIRE *next to her.* FERGUS *sits in the back.*

FERGUS: So it was you all the time.

MAGUIRE: Who'd you think it was?

FERGUS: I thought it was Dave.

MAGUIRE: And who's Dave when he's at home?

FERGUS: He's at home.

MAGUIRE: Should blow you away, you know that?

FERGUS: I know that.

[MAGUIRE *stubs his cigarette out on* FERGUS's *hand, then whacks him on the teeth with his closed fist.*]

MAGUIRE: I'm getting emotional. And I don't want to get fucking emotional – you understand, Hennessy?

FERGUS: I understand.

MAGUIRE: Fuck you, too –

[JUDE *drives.* FERGUS *looks through the back window at the street outside.*]

JUDE: Leave him alone, Peter. He's in love.

MAGUIRE: That true, Fergus? You in love?

FERGUS: Absolutely.

MAGUIRE: And what's she like between the sheets?

FERGUS: Definitely unusual.

MAGUIRE: And who is she?

FERGUS: Just a girl.

MAGUIRE: And you know what'll happen if you fuck up again, don't you?

FERGUS: Aye, I do, Peter.

MAGUIRE: Good.

[*The car pulls off.*]

EXTERIOR. REGENCY SQUARE – NIGHT.

The car draws to a halt in a sedate square. Several doors down is the entrance to what looks like a sedate conservative club.

In the car, MAGUIRE *turns off the engine. He nods toward the building.*

MAGUIRE: So what do you think that is, Hennessy?

FERGUS: A hotel?

MAGUIRE: It's a knocking-shop. *Très* discreet, huh?

MAGUIRE: He visits his ladies on Tuesday and Thursday nights and Saturday mornings. His security's in the car beyond.
[*He nods toward a car, a Daimler, parked some distance away.* FERGUS *looks from the window to the car.*]

FERGUS: Who is he?

MAGUIRE: Doesn't matter who he is. He is what we would call a legitimate target.

FERGUS: Thank God for that.

MAGUIRE: You being cynical, Hennessy?

FERGUS: Hope not.

MAGUIRE: Good. So what do you think?

FERGUS: Whoever hits him'll be hit, if those men are any good. And I presume you can't get in.

MAGUIRE: Right.

FERGUS: So it's on the street.

MAGUIRE: Right.

FERGUS: Kind of suicide, isn't it?
[JUDE *turns around to look at him.*]

FERGUS: But, then, I don't have a choice.

JUDE: Och, you do, Fergie.

FERGUS: Of course. I forgot.

JUDE: Come on, Fergie. A rehearsal.
[JUDE *and* FERGUS *get out of the car. They walk down the street, down from the brothel-cum-club, where there is a café-bar with some tables.*]

EXTERIOR. REGENCY SQUARE – NIGHT.

FERGUS *and* JUDE, *crossing the street.*

JUDE: You keep your mind on the job, boy –

FERGUS: And then you'll leave her out of it?

JUDE: Aye. Then we'll leave her be.
[*They take their seats by the tables. We can see the brothel down the way.*]

JUDE: He's arthritic. Takes him three minutes to get to the door.

[*She checks her watch.* FERGUS *is sweating.*]

FERGUS: And what if I say no?

JUDE: You know what. Go.

[*Down by the brothel, the door swings open.*]

[FERGUS *walks like any pedestrian down toward the brothel. There is an old, portly gent in a city suit emerging from it. The car by the pavement kicks into action and the door opens.*]

[FERGUS *quickens his pace.*]

[JUDE, *by the café, watches.*]

[FERGUS, *walking.*]

[*The* GENT *makes his way, with gout-ridden slowness, across the pavement, through the passersby, toward the car.*]

[*A burly security* MAN *emerging from the car, walking toward the old* GENT.]

[FERGUS *reaches the car just before he does, and passes between him and the open door. The old* GENT'*s stomach brushes* FERGUS'*s elbow.*]

GENT: Pardon me, young man —

[FERGUS *walks on.*]

[JUDE, *from the café, watches* — FERGUS *walking on, the old* MAN *being eased with painstaking care inside the Daimler. Then the door closing and the Daimler pulling off.*]

[*When the Daimler has passed* FERGUS, *he turns around and walks back.*]

[JUDE *smiles and leaps up as he approaches.*]

JUDE: You were made for this.

FERGUS: Was I?

JUDE: Perfect.

FERGUS: And what happens then?

JUDE: We'll be on the other side. We'll move when you do.

FERGUS: And what if you don't?

JUDE: Fergus, I think you don't trust me.

FERGUS: You may be right.

JUDE: Stay late at your work tomorrow night and I'll bring you the gear.

[JUDE *begins to walk away.*]

FERGUS: Jude?

JUDE: Yes?

FERGUS: Who's the old geezer?

JUDE: Some judge . . .

[*She walks off, crosses the road to* MAGUIRE, *in the car.* FERGUS *turns around to see* DIL, *in front of the café. She goes inside; he follows.*]

FERGUS: Why'd you follow me, Dil?

DIL: Was jealous, Jimmy.

[*She downs a drink and motions for another. She seems high.*]

FERGUS: Shouldn't be, Dil.

DIL: Why shouldn't I be jealous?

[*There are tears streaming down her face. He takes his hand and begins to wipe her face.*]

DIL: Don't. My makeup.

DIL: She own you, Jimmy?

FERGUS: Yes.

DIL: She from Scotland too?

FERGUS: You could say that.

DIL: And you're not going to tell me more?

FERGUS: I can't.

[*He wipes the tears from her face with a tissue then dabs the tissue in her drink and wipes some more.*]

DIL: What you doing, Jimmy?

FERGUS: I'm not sure.

DIL: Do you like me even a little bit?

FERGUS: More than that.

FERGUS: Come for a walk . . .

[*She allows herself be led out.*]

EXTERIOR. HAIR SALON – NIGHT.

DIL *and* FERGUS *walking.* FERGUS *stops her by the window.*

FERGUS: You do something for me, Dil?

DIL: Anything.

FERGUS: You'd do anything for me?

DIL: Afraid so.

FERGUS: You got the keys to the shop?

[*They walk inside.*]

INTERIOR. HAIR SALON – NIGHT.

DIL *and* FERGUS *standing in the darkness.*

DIL: You want another haircut, baby?

FERGUS: No. Sit down.

[*He sits her down in one of the chairs.*]

FERGUS: You'd do anything for me?

DIL: Anything.

[DIL *nods.* FERGUS *takes up a scissors to snip at her hair. Her head leaps back.*]

DIL: No way –

FERGUS: You said anything, Dil –

DIL: A girl has to draw the line somewhere –

FERGUS: Want to change you to a man, Dil . . .

[*She stares at him.*]

DIL: Why?

FERGUS: It's a secret.

DIL: You'd like me better that way, Jimmy?

FERGUS: Yes.

DIL: And you wouldn't leave me?

FERGUS: No.

DIL: You promise.

FERGUS: I promise.

[*She takes a breath.*]

DIL: Go on, then.

[FERGUS *begins to cut.*]

[*Close-up on* DIL's *face as her hair is shorn. Tears stream down her cheeks.*]

DIL: You're no good at this, Jimmy.

FERGUS: I'm sorry.

[*But he keeps cutting. He gives* DIL *a short, cropped military cut like* JODY's.]

DIL: You want to make me look like him . . .

FERGUS: No. Want to make you into something new. That nobody recognizes . . .

[*She looks in the mirror at it in the dark.*]

DIL: Don't recognize myself, Jimmy.

INTERIOR. DIL'S FLAT – NIGHT.

DIL *enters, with her new haircut. She goes to turn on the light. He stops her hand.*

FERGUS: Don't.

[*She looks at her hand on his.*]

FERGUS: Better in the dark.

[*Her fingers close around his.*]

DIL: So it's true, then?

FERGUS: What?

DIL: You like me better like this.

FERGUS: Yes.

[*She brings her lips to his neck. He lets them stay there. His hands travel up to her blouse. He begins to undo the buttons.*]

DIL: Oh, Jimmy –

[*Slowly the blouse slips down, exposing her male torso. She falls down to her knees and tugs at his belt.*]

FERGUS: Dil . . . get up . . .

[*He raises her to her feet and leads her toward the bed. She stretches languorously down on it. He unzips her skirt slowly, and draws it off. She turns on the bed sexily, her face to the mattress. She is wearing suspender-belts underneath her skirt.*]

DIL: Baby . . .

[*But* FERGUS *stands and walks quietly over to the wardrobe where the soldier's things are.* DIL, *on the bed, slowly turns.*]

DIL: Honey . . .

[*We see* FERGUS *from her point of view, coming toward her with Jody's white cricket shirt, glowing eerily in the dark.*]

FERGUS: Don't call me that –

DIL: Sorry. What you doing?

[FERGUS *draws her slowly up to a standing position.*]

FERGUS: Try this on, Dil.

[*He wraps the shirt around her.*]

DIL: Why?

FERGUS: For me.

DIL: For you . . .

[*She kisses him.*]

EXTERIOR. SMALL HOTEL – NIGHT.

FERGUS *leading* DIL, *dressed in Jody's cricket clothes, down the street and inside.*
DIL: Why are we going here, Jimmy?
FERGUS: Look on it like a honeymoon.

INTERIOR. SMALL HOTEL ROOM – NIGHT.

From above, we see the figures of FERGUS *and* DIL, *sleeping on a double bed, both fully clothed.*
  Time lapse. The light gradually fills the room. FERGUS *wakes. Looks at the bedside clock, and very gingerly rises, puts on his coat, and walks out.*

EXTERIOR. SITE – EVENING.

A car pulls up at the site. JUDE *gets out. She has a satchel in her hand.*

INTERIOR. SITE – EVENING.

FERGUS *looking down a ladder-staircase at* JUDE.
JUDE: You a handyman, Fergie?
FERGUS: I take pride in my work.
JUDE: I sincerely hope so.
  [FERGUS *climbs down a ladder to* JUDE; *she hands him something.*]
JUDE: Tools of the trade.
  [*She kisses him.* FERGUS *looks at her expressionlessly.*]
JUDE: And forget about the girl.
  [FERGUS *opens what* JUDE *has given him – looking inside. There is a gun wrapped in an oilcloth.*]

INTERIOR. SMALL HOTEL – NIGHT.

FERGUS *enters. The room is empty. He calls.*
FERGUS: Dil?

[*No reply. He runs outside.*]

EXTERIOR. DIL'S PLACE – NIGHT.

FERGUS *looks up at her building, but the lights are off in her flat. The sound of feet behind him. He turns and sees* DIL *walking toward him, a bottle in her hand. He runs toward her.*

FERGUS: Dil! Dil! What the fuck are you doing here?

DIL: I'm going home!

FERGUS: Told you to stay in the hotel!

DIL: Thought you was fooling me. Thought you was leaving me.
   [*They are tussling in the darkness of the park. She is very drunk.*]

FERGUS: I had to go to work!

DIL: Stayed all day in that room thinking every noise was you. There's something you're not telling me, Jimmy.
   [*He takes her arm.*]

FERGUS: Come on . . .

DIL: No! I'm going home . . .
   [FERGUS *and* DIL, *on the stairs up to* DIL's *flat.*]

DIL: So tell me.

FERGUS: I was trying to get out of something.

DIL: No! Tell me everything, Jimmy.
   [FERGUS *looks at her.*]

FERGUS: You got to forget you ever saw me, Dil.

DIL: You mean that?

FERGUS: Yes.
   [*And she suddenly faints into his arms. As if on cue.*]

FERGUS: Stop it, would you?
   [*There is no response. He shakes her.*]

FERGUS: Give over, Dil, for fuck's sake –
   [*Still no response. He grows alarmed. He slaps her cheek. She opens her eyes slowly.*]

DIL: Sorry. I get nervous. I got this blood condition. Just help me inside Jimmy, then I'll be all right.

INTERIOR. DIL'S FLAT – NIGHT.

He walks in holding her. Leans her against the wall, then goes to the window to check the street outside.

    She takes a large slug from a bottle of whiskey.

FERGUS: You heard what I said, Dil?

DIL: My pills . . .

    [*She points weakly to a cabinet through the open door of the bathroom.*]

FERGUS: What pills?

DIL: Prescription. For my condition.

FERGUS: What condition?

DIL: My condition. Ennui.

    [*He goes and gets the pills.*]

    [*She takes a handful of pills. She drinks from the whiskey bottle.*]

FERGUS: Are you supposed to take that many?

DIL: Only in times of extreme stress.

    [*She walks around the room, drinking, then sits down.*]

DIL: See, they all say good-bye sometime. 'Cept for him.

    [*She looks at the picture of* JODY. *Then she looks at* FERGUS.]

FERGUS: Are you all right, Dil?

DIL: I will be.

    [*She stares straight ahead, the bottle clutched in her hands between her knees.*]

DIL: Go on, then.

    [FERGUS *walks slowly toward the door.*]

FERGUS: Good-bye Dil.

DIL: Jimmy?

FERGUS: What?

DIL: Don't go like that.

    [*She looks at him, standing up. Something incredibly attractive about her.*]

DIL: Can't help what I am.

FERGUS: Can't help what I am.

    [*He walks slowly toward her. He kisses her, on the lips.*]

    [*We see the photograph with the soldier's smiling face.* FERGUS *looks from it to her. She seems to be in a sweet narcotic haze.*

She reaches out her hand and strokes his.]

DIL: Knew you had a heart . . .

[FERGUS *sits down on the bed.* DIL *is lying back on it.*]

FERGUS: Dil. Can I tell you something? I knew your man.

DIL: You knew which man?

FERGUS: Your soldier.

DIL: You knew my Jody?

[*She still strokes his hand. Her voice is dreamily slurred, her eyes far away.*]

FERGUS: Lifted him from a carnival in Belfast. Held him hostage for three days.

DIL: You knew my Jody?

FERGUS: Are you listening?

[DIL *smiles woozily.*]

DIL: Yes.

FERGUS: I got the order to shoot him. Before I could do it he ran. Ran into a tank and died.

DIL: Died . . .

FERGUS: Did you hear me?

DIL: You killed my Jody?

FERGUS: In a manner of speaking.

DIL: It was you . . .

[*She is not rational. She is smiling, far away somewhere.*]

FERGUS: You should scream. You should beat my head off.

[*She woozily tries to hit him round the face.*]

DIL: You killed my Jody.

FERGUS: No.

DIL: You didn't.

FERGUS: I suppose I tried.

DIL: You tried.

FERGUS: Don't you want to kill me?

[DIL *raises an unsteady hand and points it at him.*]

DIL: Bang . . .

[*He strokes her cheek. She says very slowly and sleepily:*]

DIL: Don't leave me tonight. Might kill me, too.

FERGUS: Okay.

[*Her eyes close. She falls into a deep sleep.* FERGUS *looks down at her, almost fondly.*]

INTERIOR. DIL'S PLACE – MORNING.

They are lying on the bed together, fully clothed. DIL *wakes. She rises very quietly and goes to his coat, thrown across a chair. She searches through the pockets and takes out the gun.*

INTERIOR.

JUDE *in bed. An alarm sounds; she reaches to turn it off.*

INTERIOR. DIL'S FLAT.

DIL *takes several silk stockings out of a drawer and ties them very securely to each corner of the brass bed. She ties them round both of* FERGUS's *feet, very gently, so as not to wake him.*

INTERIOR. ROOM.

JUDE, *in front of a mirror, getting ready.*

INTERIOR. DIL'S FLAT.

She draws one of FERGUS's *hands up, very gingerly, and ties that securely to the upright. She ties the other and is drawing it upward when he wakes. She jerks the silk stocking so it is secure.*
FERGUS: What the fuck –
  [DIL *speaks unnaturally quietly.*]
DIL: So tell me what you're doing, Jimmy.

INTERIOR. HOTEL ROOM – MORNING.

JUDE, *fully dressed. She takes a gun wrapped in a plastic bag from under the bed and slips it in her handbag.*

INTERIOR. DIL'S FLAT – MORNING.

DIL *crouching beside* FERGUS, *his gun in her hand.*
DIL: Didn't really listen last night. I heard but I didn't listen.

[FERGUS, *staring at her. He tries to pull on the bindings*.]

DIL: Won't do you no good. Dil knows how to tie a body.

[*She stands up, still pointing the gun at* FERGUS.]

DIL: Wondered why you came on to me like that when you gave me the look.

FERGUS: He asked me to see were you all right.

EXTERIOR. STREET – DAY.

JUDE *on the street.* MAGUIRE*'s car pulls up rapidly and she gets inside.*

DIL: See, I fix on anyone that's nice to me. Just the littlest bit nice and I'm yours.

FERGUS: Stop it, Dil –

DIL: Just don't kick Dil and she'll be touched. Be nice to her and she'll be yours forever.

[*She looks at him, tears in her eyes*.]

DIL: See, I should blow you away, Jimmy. But I can't do that. Yet.

FERGUS: Let me go, Dil.

[*He drags at his bindings*.]

DIL: Why?

FERGUS: Got to be somewhere.

DIL: Try and go, then.

EXTERIOR. STREET BY BROTHEL – DAY.

The figure of the JUDGE *in the window. Outline of a* WOMAN. JUDE *and* MAGUIRE *are in the car, parked across the street. They look toward the paper seller.*

MAGUIRE: Where the fuck is he? Christ –

[*He pulls furiously at his bindings*.]

FERGUS: Let me fucking go, Dil – or they'll be here –

DIL: Let them come then.

IN THE CAR. OUTSIDE BROTHEL.

JUDE: Can't stay here, Peter – drive around once more –

[*He drives off*.]

[FERGUS *collapsed back on the bed, exhausted.*]
DIL: Just want your company for a little while longer . . .

EXTERIOR. STREET BY BROTHEL – DAY.

MAGUIRE's *car driving round once more. No sign of* FERGUS.
MAGUIRE: That fucker's dead –
JUDE: No, we are.

INTERIOR. DIL'S FLAT – DAY.

FERGUS *strains and roars from the bed.*
FERGUS: You don't know what you're doing, Dil –
DIL: Never did . . .
  [*POV – the brothel door opening. The elderly gent* JUDGE
  comes out. The car with his SECURITY MEN *guns up.*]
MAGUIRE: Give me the shooter, Jude –
JUDE: You're crazy –
MAGUIRE: Give me it –
  [*He grabs it from her pocket. Throws open the door and runs
  across the street.* JUDE *dives into the driver's seat.*

INTERIOR. DIL'S FLAT.

FERGUS, *pulling at his bindings.*

EXTERIOR. OUTSIDE THE BROTHEL.

The JUDGE *walking toward the open door of the car, held open by
his* GOON. MAGUIRE, *running toward him, gun in hand. The*
GOON *sees him.* MAGUIRE *shoots as he runs. Once, twice, three
times, four. The* JUDGE *falls. The* GOON, *hit in the arm, pulls an
Uzi and returns fire.* MAGUIRE *hit, still shooting. Other* GOONS
tear from the car. Mayhem, screaming. JUDE *hits the pedal on her
car and screeches off.* MAGUIRE, *dead.*

INTERIOR. DIL'S FLAT – DAY.

DIL, *dressed in the soldier's cricket clothes. She looks like a sweet little boy. She places a cassette in the tape deck – 'The Crying Game' song. She comes to the bed, and points the gun at* FERGUS's *head.*

DIL: You like me now, Jimmy?

FERGUS: I like you, Dil.

DIL: Give me a bit more, baby, a bit more.

FERGUS: More what?

DIL: More endearments.

FERGUS: I like you, Dil.

DIL: Love me.

FERGUS: Yes.

DIL: Tell me you love me.

FERGUS: Whatever you say, Dil.

DIL: Then say it.

FERGUS: Love you, Dil.

DIL: You do?

FERGUS: Yeah.

DIL: What would you do for me?

FERGUS: Anything.

[*She begins to cry and lays the gun gently on his chest.*]

DIL: Say it again.

FERGUS: I'd do anything for you, Dil.

[*She pulls on his bindings to release him.*]

EXTERIOR. STREET.

Two police cars, sirens wailing.

INTERIOR. DIL'S FLAT.

DIL's *face, close to* FERGUS's, *as the stockings that bound his hands are nearly undone.*

DIL: And you'll never leave me?

FERGUS: Never.

DIL: I know you're lying, Jimmy, but it's nice to hear it.

[*His arm is free. He strokes her hair.*]

FERGUS: I'm sorry, Dil.

[*She shudders with weeping. The music of the song plays in the background.*]

[*The door,* JUDE *walking through the door, arms extended, holding a gun.*]

JUDE: You stupid shit –

JUDE: Once was bad enough. But twice.

[DIL *rises from the bed and points her gun at* JUDE.]

DIL: You didn't knock, honey –

[DIL *fires, hits* JUDE. JUDE *falls and is writhing on the floor.*]

FERGUS: Dil!

JUDE: Get that thing off me, Fergus –

[DIL *walks closer, holding the gun and pointing it at* JUDE.]

DIL: What was that she called you, Jimmy?

FERGUS: Fergus.

DIL: What's Fergus?

FERGUS: It's my name, Dil.

DIL: What happened to Jimmy?

JUDE: I said get it off me, Fergus –

[JUDE *staggers toward her gun. Manages to grab it.*]

DIL: What's she going to do, Jimmy? She going to blow you away?

[DIL *shoots again, like a child, playing with a toy. She hits* JUDE *in her gun shoulder.* JUDE *spins one way, the gun the other.*]

DIL: Was she there too? When you got my Jody?

[FERGUS *screams:*]

FERGUS: Dil!!!

DIL: I asked you a question, honey – were you there too –

JUDE: You sick bitch –

[*As she raises the gun,* DIL *shoots her repeatedly, saying:*]

DIL: You was there, wasn't you? You used those tits and that ass to get him, didn't you?

[FERGUS *screams from the bed. He rips free his other arm.* DIL *shoots* JUDE *in the throat, and she falls dead, covered in blood.* DIL *turns the gun on* FERGUS.]

DIL: She was there, wasn't she?

FERGUS: She was –

67

DIL: And she used her tits and that cute little ass to get him, didn't she?

FERGUS: Yes.

DIL: Tell me what she wore.

FERGUS: Can't remember . . .

[DIL *points the gun at him, squeezing on the trigger. Then she stops.*]

DIL: Can't do it, Jimmy. He won't let me.

[*She looks at the picture; walks over and sits down in front of it.*]

DIL: You won't let me, Jody —

[*She raises the gun and places it in her mouth.* FERGUS *takes it gently from her mouth and places it on the table. He lifts her up by the shoulders.*]

FERGUS: You've got to go now, Dil.

DIL: Do I?

FERGUS: Yes. Now.

DIL: Am I in trouble, Jimmy?

FERGUS: Not if you go.

DIL: Will I see you again?

FERGUS: You will, Dil.

DIL: Promise?

FERGUS: I promise.

DIL: Where am I to go, Jimmy?

FERGUS: The Metro.

DIL: Meet Col.

FERGUS: Yes. Say hello to Col.

[*He leads her out the door.* FERGUS *goes back into the room, past* JUDE's *body. Looks out the window to where he can see* DIL, *staggering down the street, through the crowds that have gathered. The wail of police sirens coming closer. He watches* DIL *walk, with her funny walk, until she vanishes among the crowd. Then looks down and sees the cop cars pushing through the knot of people around the house. He picks up the gun, wipes it with a rag to remove* DIL's *fingerprints. He picks up the gun and turns to the picture of the soldier; talks to it.*]

FERGUS: You should have stayed at home.

[*He sits in the chair by the window, waiting.*]

[*Fade to black.*]

INTERIOR. PRISON VISITING ROOM – DAY.

Fade up to reveal a large interior, with light streaming in the windows. Large barred doors open and a group of WOMEN *come through, with parcels,* CHILDREN *in tow, etc. Among them is* DIL, *looking resplendent. She walks past the rows of* CONVICTS *with their families, up to a glass cage, where* FERGUS *sits, waiting.*]

DIL: Got you the multivitamins and the iron tablets hon –

FERGUS: Don't call me that –

DIL: Sorry, love. Now, the white ones are magnesium supplement –

FERGUS: Stop it, Dil –

DIL: I've got to keep you healthy, Jimmy. I'm counting the days. Two thousand three hundred and thirty-four left.

FERGUS: Thirty-five.

DIL: I'm sorry, darling. I keep forgetting the leap year. What am I supposed to call you then, Jimmy?

FERGUS: Fergus.

DIL: Fergus. Fergus my love, light of my life –

FERGUS: Please, Dil.

DIL: Can't help it. You're doing time for me. No greater love, as the man says. Wish you'd tell me why.

FERGUS: As the man said, it's in my nature.

DIL: What's that supposed to mean?

[*She shakes her head.*]

FERGUS: Well, there was this scorpion, you see. And he wants to go across the river. But he couldn't swim. So he went to this frog, who can swim and he says to him, 'Excuse me, Mr Froggy . . .'

[*Camera pulls back, and as* FERGUS *tells the story of the scorpion and the frog, the music comes up – 'Stand By Your Man'.*]

THE END